DEFACING THE MONUMENT

[redacted]

DEFACING THE

[redacted]

PRAISE FOR

DEFACING THE MONUMENT

DEFACING THE MONUMENT ELUCIDATES THE POWERFUL WAYS THAT POETRY has documented the present and the absent, the visible and the invisible, the broken and the breaking. Susan Briante's investigations thread through borderlands, languages, genres and discourses to show that our words and poems and bodies always emerge in relation to the violence of the state, the violence of the bank, the violence of those who purchase, who silence, who deport. Poetry can mean something in the public sphere, though the poets don't always believe this. Here are poetries that exemplify this by archiving the erased and the eraser, the consumed and the consumer, the authoritarian bodies and those they seek to destroy.

—Daniel Borzutzky

IIIII

I FELT SO INTELLECTUALLY AND EMOTIONALLY NOURISHED WHILE READING Susan Briante's *Defacing the Monument*. Briante not only attributes, but asks why we must attribute; gives witness accounts but questions who she is as witness. Briante, with such incredible care and generosity, investigates every frame that contains stories of suffering; every platitude that proves our moral certitude. By laying bare these limitations, Briante breaks open possibilities where injustice can be "newly felt." Not only that, she asks how poetry can be a social practice and not just a feat of imagination. Anyone who's interested in writing about someone other than themselves needs to read this book. *Defacing the Monument* is a stunning and brilliant intervention on how poetry documents history.

—Cathy Park Hong

MON
UM
ENT

SUSAN BRIANTE

NOEMI PRESS
BLACKSBURG, VIRGINIA

INFIDEL POETICS
#5

design: Douglas Kearney
text set in Alda OT CEV + Fira Sans Condensed; display in Futura
published by Noemi Press, Inc.
A Nonprofit Literary Organization.

www.noemipress.org

Fifty percent of the royalties from the sale of the book will be donated to the Kino Border Initiative, a binational migrant aid and advocacy organization.

IIII IIII IIII IIII IIII IIII IIII IIII IIII IIII

TABLE OF CONTENTS

What happens when we attempt to interrupt a war machine, turning it against itself? What occurs when we divert a language of hemispheric reterritorialization, embodied in an agreement like NAFTA/TLC? We encounter a delirious epistemology which, even when suspended, does not cease to manifest something: that which does not appear to have a place in the predetermined language of politics and poetry. Even in the very suspension of its logic, the document thinks against itself.

—Hugo García Manríquez

IIII

The successful documentary poem withstands the pressure of reality to remain a poem in its own right: its language and form cannot be reduced to an ephemeral poster, ready made for its moment but headed for the recycling bin. While it may be that such poems will not "stand up" in a court of law, they testify to the often unheard voices of people struggling to survive in the face of unspeakable violence....These poems ride the ambiguity between a nothing and a something that can be used. Their power resides in their negotiation between language of evidence and language of transcendence.

—Philip Metres

IIII

The popular perception is that art is apart. I insist it is part of.

—CD Wright

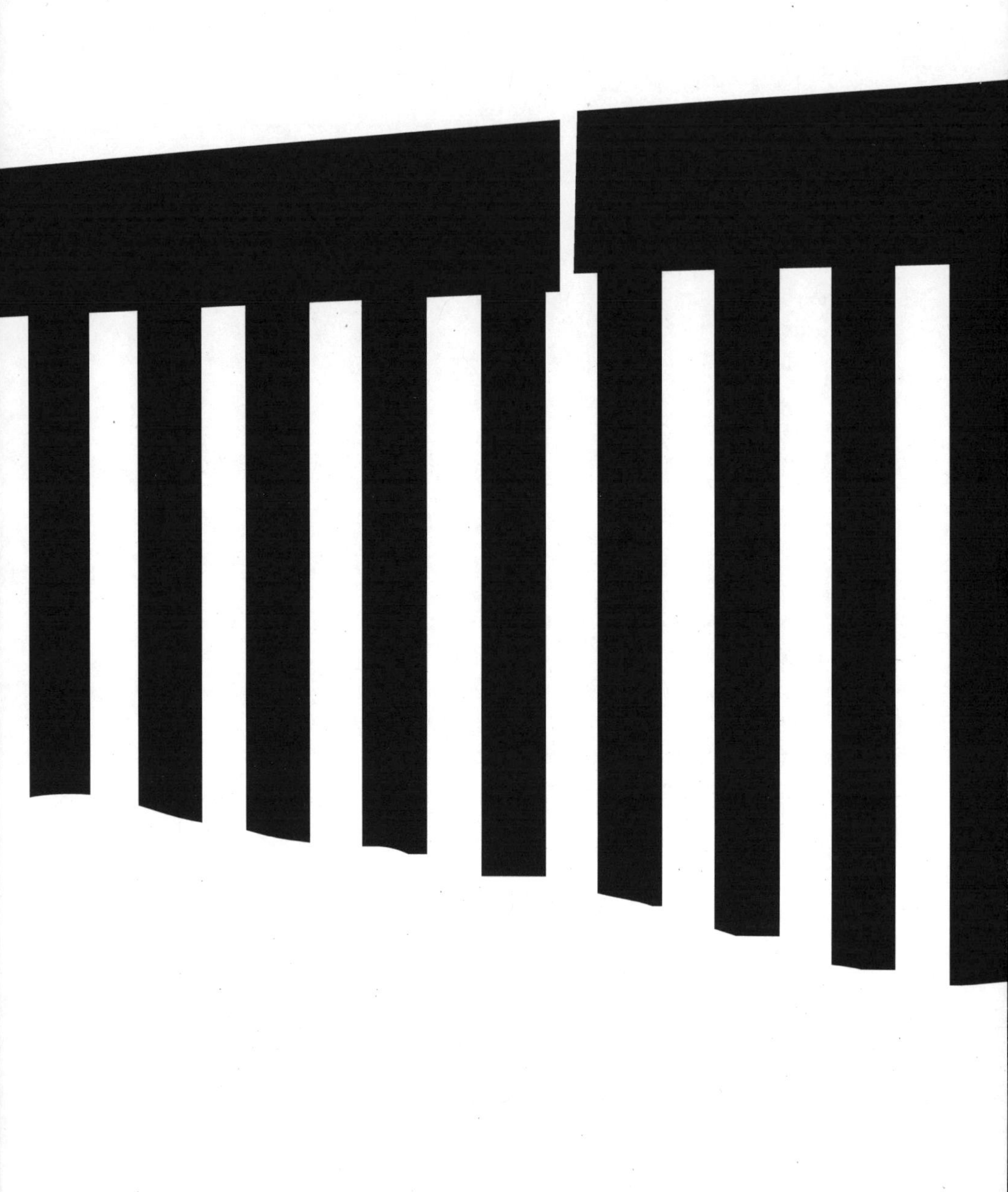

FRAMES, ERASURÉS, GRAFFITI

Why don't ya have scat

Yes a little

BEFORE HONORABLE ERIC J. MARKOVICH
OPERATION STREAMLINE
SPECIAL PROCEEDINGS COURTROOM - 2nd FLOOR
Tuesday, September 26, 2017

1

he is very nervous

COURTESY DRAFT COPY

17-27739MP [redacted]
DOA: 09/24/2017
ATTY Rodolfo Valenzuela (CJA)
TRUE NAME:
8 USC 1325(a)(1) ILLEGAL ENTRY
Speaks English: No

Thinking clearly today - si
Are u pleading guilty vol + of you own free will
pause si
no shackles

17-27741MP [redacted]
DOA: 09/24/2017
ATTY Micaela Portillo (CJA)
TRUE NAME:
8 USC 1325(a)(1) ILLEGAL ENTRY
Speaks English: No

9/24 - Nogales
6 months
think clear + are you pleading guilty - Yes
has anyone promised ya anything to get ya to plead guilty
do you under the offense - yes

17-27742MP [redacted]
DOA: 09/25/2017
ATTY Raymond Panzarella (CJA)
TRUE NAME:
8 USC 1325(a)(1) ILLEGAL ENTRY
Speaks English: No

yes - clear head
yes - volun + of yr own free will
do you under the offense - yes -
do you under consequences - yes

17-27743MP [redacted] ✓
DOA: 09/25/2017
ATTY Joe Machado (CJA)
TRUE NAME:
8 USC 1325(a)(1) ILLEGAL ENTRY
Speaks English: No

9/23
Lukeville w/o Port of entr
guilty

17-27744MP [redacted]
DOA: 09/25/2017
ATTY Vincent Lacsamana (CJA)
TRUE NAME:
8 USC 1325(a)(1) ILLEGAL ENTRY
Speaks English: No

17-27748MP [redacted]
DOA: 09/25/2017
ATTY Thomas Jacobs (CJA)
TRUE NAME:
8 USC 1325(a)(1) ILLEGAL ENTRY
Speaks English: No

17-27750MP [redacted] *
DOA: 09/25/2017
ATTY Alfred Islas (CJA)
TRUE NAME:
8 USC 1325(a)(1) ILLEGAL ENTRY
Speaks English: No

9/22
Sasabe
yes
guilty

Short blue shirt

4 microphones

Did you enter the US w/immig doc or did you walk through the desert?

4Runner
SONORA
243-SYZ-2
BVB6104

2 The word "economic" does not appear in the text of the Department of Homeland Security's webpage entitled "Obtaining Asylum in the United States,"

is not uttered into the court record.

The word "economic" remains in my mouth at the back of the courtroom, where I sit scribbling on a legal pad, trying to trace a relation to the seven men who stand before the judge shackled at the wrists, waists, and ankles.[1]

The body is a condition—the nation another.

I used to believe the document tethered the poem to the earth, to soil that one could taste, that could be nutrient to more than one.

But a document can pull a nation out from under you.

In the US District Court, Arizona District, shackles chime like the rigging of a ship in harbor in the moments before a voyage. Seven men approach the bench, one by one they speak directly into the microphone

to become a name in a document, a few words in the record, and one syllable of consent.

3 *Do you understand the rights that you are giving up, the consequences of pleading guilty and the terms of your written plea agreement? Are you pleading guilty voluntarily and of your own free will? Are you a citizen of the United States? On or about March 17, 2017 did you enter the United States from Mexico near Nogales without coming through a designated port of entry? How do you plead to the charge of illegal entry?*

Do you understand the rights that you are giving up, the consequences of pleading guilty and the terms of your written plea agreement? Are you pleading guilty voluntarily and of your own free will? Are you a citizen of the United States? On or about March 18, 2017 did you enter the United States from Mexico near Lukeville without coming through a designated port of entry? How do you plead to the charge of illegal entry?

Do you understand the rights that you are giving up, the consequences of pleading guilty and the terms of your written plea agreement? Are you pleading guilty voluntarily and of your own free will? Are you a citizen of the United States? On or about March 14, 2017 did you enter the United States from Mexico near Sasabe without coming through a designated port of entry? How do you plead to the charge of illegal entry?

Do you understand the rights that you are giving up, the consequences of pleading guilty and the terms of your written plea agreement? Are you pleading guilty voluntarily and of your own free will? Are you a citizen of the United States? On or about March 18, 2017 did you enter the United States from Mexico near Nogales without coming through a designated port of entry? How do you plead to the charge of illegal entry?

Do you understand the rights that you are giving up, the consequences of pleading guilty and the terms of your written plea agreement? Are you pleading guilty voluntarily and of your own free will? Are you a citizen of the United States? On or about March 15, 2017 did you enter the United States from Mexico near Sasabe without coming through a designated port of entry? How do you plead to the charge of illegal entry?

Do you understand the rights that you are giving up, the consequences of pleading guilty and the terms of your written plea agreement? Are you pleading guilty voluntarily and of your own free will? Are you a citizen of the United States? On or about March 17, 2017 did you enter the United States from Mexico near Lukeville without coming through a designated port of entry? How do you plead to the charge of illegal entry?

Do you understand the rights that you are giving up, the consequences of pleading guilty and the terms of your written plea agreement? Are you pleading guilty voluntarily and of your own free will? Are you a citizen of the United States? On or about March 14, 2017 did you enter the United States from Mexico near Nogales without coming through a designated port of entry? How do you plead to the charge of illegal entry?

4 In an endnote to her serial poem "The Book of the Dead" about the murderous exploitation of miners in Gauley Bridge, West Virginia, Muriel Rukeyser wrote: "Poetry can extend the document."

For Rukeyser, poetry became a tool to expand the documentary record, because the profits of Union Carbide, the parent company responsible for the gross negligence that lead to the silicosis poisoning and deaths of anywhere from 764 to 2,000 miners, the majority of whom were African American migrant workers, did not appear in the Congressional testimony about the events,

because centuries of systemic racism did not appear in Congressional testimony or newspaper reports on the "disaster."

Rukeyser wanted to situate primary documentary evidence against eyewitness accounts and interviews as well as within larger systemic forces and legacies in order to make clear that the Gauley Bridge "disaster" was not an exception,

but rather another coordinate in a long trajectory of white supremacy and exploitative capitalism.

I summon Rukeyser now because the words "economic," "family," and "asylum" do not appear on the court calendar on the days I attend the Operation Streamline hearings, are not uttered into the court records,

because the salary of the private prison corporation lobbyist is absent from the record as well.

When Rukeyser writes "poetry can extend the document," she suggests that the poem can account for a document's limits as well as its elisions and erasures.

The state shapes documents to articulate narratives that benefit the policies of the state, political narratives as fixed as the wall that cuts through Nogales, blacking out landscape and sky like the eyes of a person in a photograph wishing to remain anonymous, or a text redacted.

The court calendar for Operation Streamline proceedings includes the defendant's name, date of arrest, their lawyer's name, the charges they face, their English language competency. The complete calendar for the day extends 10 pages.

But it does not tell us: What spiraled and scurried in the wake of these travelers? What screamed and cried? What debt? What tender? What moans?

Most migrants are permitted to add only three words to the court record: "Yes," "no," and "guilty."

5 In 2005, Operation Streamline began the prosecution of unauthorized migrants, often sending them to prison prior to deportation. Each migrant leaves the proceedings with a criminal record.

In this sense, the process is documentary.

Immigration rights advocates have called the proceedings "assembly line justice," because as many as 75 migrants might be brought before a judge in a single day, plead guilty to the felony offense of unauthorized entry or re-entry into the United States to serve jail time or face jail time should they be caught again.

Proponents call the process a "deterrent" despite evidence that most of those caught will try to cross again. Many have family in the United States and have lived here for years prior to deportation. Others flee violence or death threats. Others flee desperate economic conditions.[2] The threat of criminal prosecution and imprisonment often compels those attempting to cross to do so in remote and dangerous terrain, increasing the risk of suffering and death, allowing our immigration policy to turn the desert into a weapon. Since Operation Streamline was first introduced, the border death rate has risen 127 percent from 52 deaths per 100,000 apprehensions to 118 deaths per 100,000 apprehensions in 2010.[3]

However, it is undeniable that the proceedings are successful in their goal: they turn migrants into criminals.

Despite the consultations with lawyers (whom the migrants meet for the first time briefly before their hearing), despite the headsets and the court interpreter, despite the judge's (sometimes) detailed statements about rights that they are giving up in order to accept the plea bargain, some migrants do not follow what is happening.

"Do you understand the consequences of pleading guilty?" the judge asks.
"Yes, I am guilty," the migrant says.

And when the judge asks the migrant why he does not understand the question, the indigenous migrant (for whom Spanish is a second language) explains: "It's too fast."

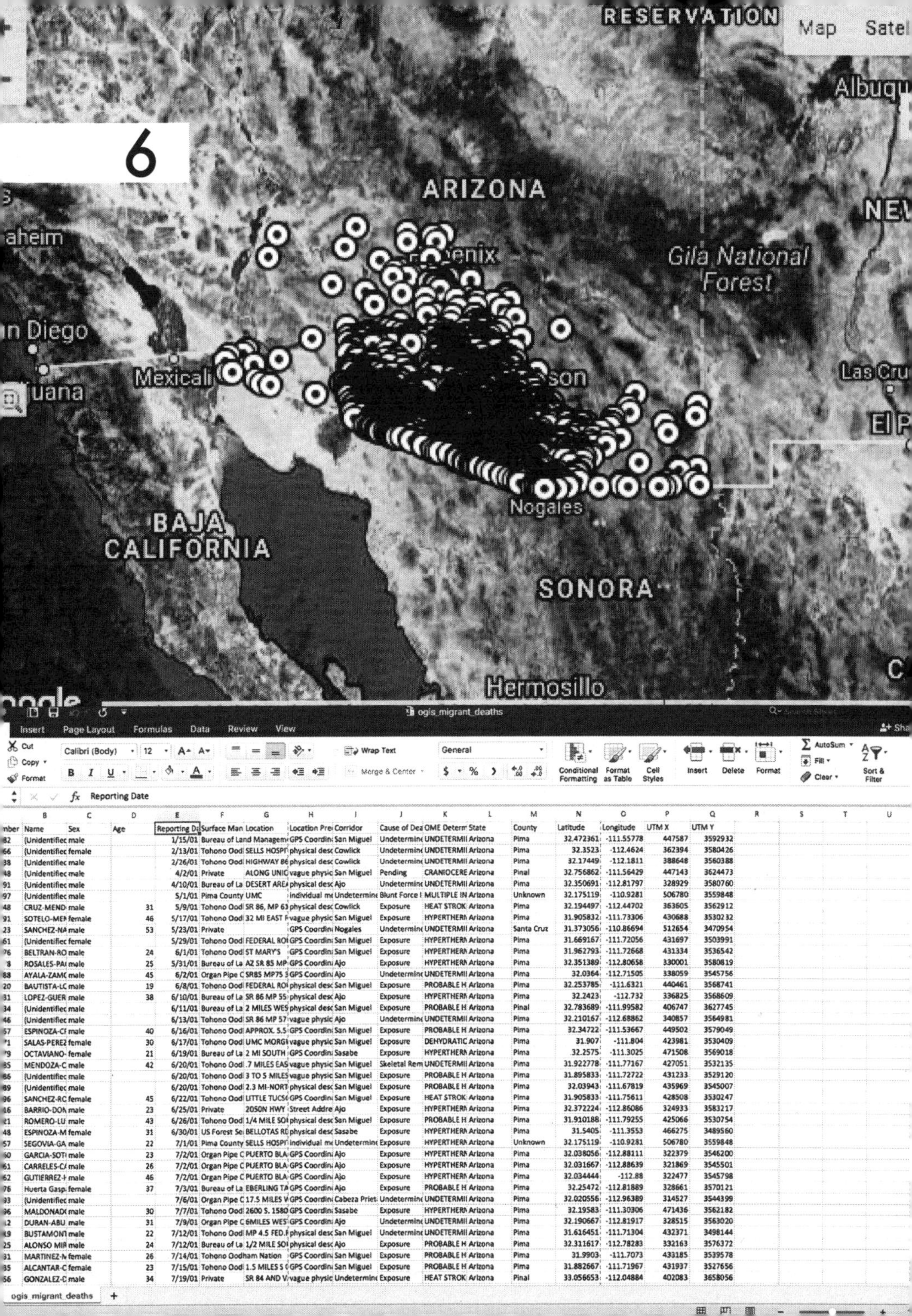

mber	Name	Sex	Age	Reporting Da	Surface Man	Location	Location Pre	Corridor	Cause of Dea	OME Determ	State	County	Latitude	Longitude	UTM X	UTM Y
82	(Unidentifiec	male		1/15/01	Bureau of Land Managem		GPS Coordin	San Miguel	Undetermin	UNDETERMII	Arizona	Pima	32.472361	-111.55778	447587	3592932
66	(Unidentifiec	female		2/13/01	Tohono Ood	SELLS HOSPI	physical desc	Cowlick	Undetermin	UNDETERMII	Arizona	Pima	32.3523	-112.4624	362394	3580426
38	(Unidentifiec	male		2/26/01	Tohono Ood	HIGHWAY 86	physical desc	Cowlick	Undetermin	UNDETERMII	Arizona	Pima	32.17449	-112.1811	388648	3560388
48	(Unidentifiec	male		4/2/01	Private	ALONG UNIC	vague physic	San Miguel	Pending	CRANIOCERE	Arizona	Pinal	32.756862	-111.56429	447143	3624473
91	(Unidentifiec	male		4/10/01	Bureau of La	DESERT AREA	physical desc	Ajo	Undetermin	UNDETERMII	Arizona	Pima	32.350691	-112.81797	328929	3580760
97	(Unidentifiec	male		5/1/01	Pima County	UMC	individual m	Undetermin	Blunt Force	MULTIPLE IN	Arizona	Unknown	32.175119	-110.9281	506780	3559848
48	CRUZ-MEND	male	31	5/9/01	Tohono Ood	SR 86, MP 63	physical desc	Cowlick	Exposure	HEAT STROK	Arizona	Pima	32.194497	-112.44702	363605	3562912
91	SOTELO-ME	female	46	5/17/01	Tohono Ood	32 MI EAST F	vague physic	San Miguel	Exposure	HYPERTHERN	Arizona	Pima	31.905832	-111.73306	430688	3530232
23	SANCHEZ-NA	male	53	5/23/01	Private		GPS Coordin	Nogales	Undetermin	UNDETERMII	Arizona	Santa Cruz	31.373056	-110.86694	512654	3470954
61	(Unidentifiec	female		5/29/01	Tohono Ood	FEDERAL RO	GPS Coordin	San Miguel	Exposure	HYPERTHERN	Arizona	Pima	31.669167	-111.72056	431697	3503991
76	BELTRAN-RO	male	24	6/1/01	Tohono Ood	ST MARY'S	GPS Coordin	San Miguel	Exposure	HYPERTHERN	Arizona	Pima	31.962793	-111.72668	431334	3536542
8	ROSALES-PA	male	25	5/31/01	Bureau of La	AZ SR 85 MP	GPS Coordin	Ajo	Exposure	HYPERTHERN	Arizona	Pima	32.351389	-112.80658	330001	3580819
88	AYALA-ZAMC	male	45	6/2/01	Organ Pipe C	SR85 MP75 3	GPS Coordin	Ajo	Undetermin	UNDETERMII	Arizona	Pima	32.0364	-112.71505	338059	3545756
20	BAUTISTA-LC	male	19	6/8/01	Tohono Ood	FEDERAL RO	physical desc	San Miguel	Exposure	PROBABLE H	Arizona	Pima	32.253785	-111.6321	440461	3568741
31	LOPEZ-GUER	male	38	6/10/01	Bureau of La	SR 86 MP 55	physical desc	Ajo	Exposure	HYPERTHERN	Arizona	Pima	32.2423	-112.732	336825	3568609
34	(Unidentifiec	male		6/11/01	Bureau of La	2 MILES WES	physical desc	San Miguel	Exposure	PROBABLE H	Arizona	Pinal	32.783689	-111.99582	406747	3627745
46	(Unidentifiec	male		6/13/01	Tohono Ood	SR 86 MP 57	vague physic	Ajo	Undetermin	UNDETERMII	Arizona	Pima	32.210167	-112.68862	340857	3564981
57	ESPINOZA-C	male	40	6/16/01	Tohono Ood	APPROX. 5.5	GPS Coordin	San Miguel	Exposure	PROBABLE H	Arizona	Pima	32.34722	-111.53667	449502	3579049
71	SALAS-PEREZ	female	30	6/17/01	Tohono Ood	UMC MORG	vague physic	San Miguel	Exposure	DEHYDRATIC	Arizona	Pima	31.907	-111.804	423981	3530409
79	OCTAVIANO-	female	21	6/19/01	Bureau of La	2 MI SOUTH	GPS Coordin	Sasabe	Exposure	HYPERTHERN	Arizona	Pima	32.2575	-111.3025	471508	3569018
85	MENDOZA-C	male	42	6/20/01	Tohono Ood	.7 MILES EAS	vague physic	San Miguel	Skeletal Rem	UNDETERMII	Arizona	Pima	31.922778	-111.77167	427051	3532135
86	(Unidentifiec	male		6/20/01	Tohono Ood	3 TO 5 MILES	vague physic	San Miguel	Exposure	PROBABLE H	Arizona	Pima	31.895833	-111.72722	431233	3529120
89	(Unidentifiec	male		6/20/01	Tohono Ood	2.3 MI-NORT	physical desc	San Miguel	Exposure	PROBABLE H	Arizona	Pima	32.03943	-111.67819	435969	3545007
96	SANCHEZ-RC	female	45	6/22/01	Tohono Ood	LITTLE TUCS	GPS Coordin	San Miguel	Exposure	HEAT STROK	Arizona	Pima	31.905833	-111.75611	428508	3530247
16	BARRIO-DON	male	23	6/25/01	Private	2050N HWY	Street Addre	Ajo	Exposure	HYPERTHERN	Arizona	Pima	32.372224	-112.86086	324933	3583217
21	ROMERO-LU	male	43	6/26/01	Tohono Ood	1/4 MILE SO	physical desc	San Miguel	Exposure	PROBABLE H	Arizona	Pima	31.910188	-111.79255	425066	3530754
48	ESPINOZA-M	female	31	6/30/01	US Forest Se	BELLOTAS RD	physical desc	Sasabe	Exposure	HYPERTHERN	Arizona	Pima	31.5405	-111.3553	466275	3489560
57	SEGOVIA-GA	male	22	7/1/01	Pima County	SELLS HOSPI	individual m	Undetermin	Exposure	HYPERTHERN	Arizona	Unknown	32.175119	-110.9281	506780	3559848
60	GARCIA-SOT	male	23	7/2/01	Organ Pipe C	PUERTO BLA	GPS Coordin	Ajo	Exposure	HYPERTHERN	Arizona	Pima	32.038056	-112.88111	322379	3546200
61	CARRELES-C	male	26	7/2/01	Organ Pipe C	PUERTO BLA	GPS Coordin	Ajo	Exposure	HYPERTHERN	Arizona	Pima	32.031667	-112.88639	321869	3545501
62	GUTIERREZ-I	male	46	7/2/01	Organ Pipe C	PUERTO BLA	GPS Coordin	Ajo	Exposure	HYPERTHERN	Arizona	Pima	32.034444	-112.88	322477	3545798
76	Huerta Gasp	female	37	7/3/01	Bureau of La	EBERLING TA	GPS Coordin	Ajo	Exposure	PROBABLE H	Arizona	Pima	32.25472	-112.81889	328661	3570121
93	(Unidentifiec	male		7/6/01	Organ Pipe C	17.5 MILES V	GPS Coordin	Cabeza Priet	Undetermin	UNDETERMII	Arizona	Pima	32.020556	-112.96389	314527	3544399
96	MALDONAD	male	30	7/7/01	Tohono Ood	2600 S. 1580	GPS Coordin	Sasabe	Exposure	HYPERTHERN	Arizona	Pima	32.19583	-111.30306	471436	3562182
12	DURAN-ABU	male	31	7/9/01	Organ Pipe C	6MILES WES	GPS Coordin	Ajo	Undetermin	UNDETERMII	Arizona	Pima	32.190667	-112.81917	328515	3563020
19	BUSTAMON	male	22	7/12/01	Tohono Ood	MP 4.5 FED.	physical desc	San Miguel	Undetermin	UNDETERMII	Arizona	Pima	31.616451	-111.71304	432371	3498144
25	ALONSO MIR	male	24	7/12/01	Bureau of La	1/2 MILE SO	physical desc	Ajo	Exposure	PROBABLE H	Arizona	Pima	32.311617	-112.78283	332163	3576372
31	MARTINEZ-N	female	26	7/14/01	Tohono Oodham Nation		GPS Coordin	San Miguel	Exposure	PROBABLE H	Arizona	Pima	31.9903	-111.7073	433185	3539578
35	ALCANTAR-C	female	23	7/15/01	Tohono Ood	1.5 MILES S	GPS Coordin	San Miguel	Exposure	PROBABLE H	Arizona	Pima	31.882667	-111.71967	431937	3527656
56	GONZALEZ-C	male	34	7/19/01	Private	SR 84 AND V	vague physic	Undetermin	Exposure	HEAT STROK	Arizona	Pinal	33.056653	-112.04884	402083	3658056

People For the American Way

Trump's America: For-Profit Prisons, Immigrant Detention and Shady Political Donations

Rio Tazewell <http://www.pfaw.org/spokespeople/rio-tazewell/> April 19, 2017

NEWS AND ANALYSIS

The Trump administration recently awarded a $110 million contract <https://www.usnews.com/news/best-states/texas/articles/2017-04-13/texas-getting-first-immigrant-lockup-built-under-trump> to the GEO Group, one of the country's largest private prison contractors, to develop and operate a new detention facility in Texas.

BEFORE HONORABLE ERIC J. MARKOVICH
OPERATION STREAMLINE
SPECIAL PROCEEDINGS COURTROOM - 2nd FLOOR
Tuesday, September 26, 2017

COURTESY DRAFT COPY

17-27739MP — 8 USC 1325(a)(1) ILLEGAL ENTRY
DOA: 09/24/2017
ATTY Rodolfo Valenzuela (CJA)
TRUE NAME: — Speaks English: No

17-27741MP — 8 USC 1325(a)(1) ILLEGAL ENTRY
DOA: 09/24/2017
ATTY Micaela Portillo (CJA)
TRUE NAME: — Speaks English: No

17-27742MP — 8 USC 1325(a)(1) ILLEGAL ENTRY
DOA: 09/25/2017
ATTY Raymond Panzarella (CJA)
TRUE NAME: — Speaks English: No

17-27743MP — 8 USC 1325(a)(1) ILLEGAL ENTRY
DOA: 09/25/2017
ATTY Jose Machado (CJA)
TRUE NAME: — Speaks English: No

17-27744MP — 8 USC 1325(a)(1) ILLEGAL ENTRY
DOA: 09/25/2017
ATTY Vincent Ladsamaria (CJA)
TRUE NAME: — Speaks English: No

17-27748MP — 8 USC 1325(a)(1) ILLEGAL ENTRY
DOA: 09/25/2017
ATTY Thomas Jacobs (CJA)
TRUE NAME: — Speaks English: No

17-27750MP — 8 USC 1325(a)(1) ILLEGAL ENTRY
DOA: 09/25/2017
ATTY Alfred Islas (CJA)
TRUE NAME: — Speaks English: No

7 If a line is a dot that went for a walk, then a wall is a line that divides

Nogales, Arizona, from Nogales, Sonora.

A deportee is a man who left his kids at a bus stop, was pulled over by the cops, could not produce a social security number and was sent first to jail, then to Nogales, Sonora, to be handed his belongings in a large ziplock bag from the Department of Homeland Security.

A frame of words can determine what one sees:

a man walks across the US-Mexico border along a partitioned walkway, a man walks across the US-Mexico border in a caged walkway, US officials escort a man across the US-Mexico border in a human cage.

And if I refer to him as a father of two.
And if I refer to him as a man.
And if I refer to him as a refugee.
And if I refer to him as a migrant.
And if I refer to him as undocumented.
And if I refer to him as a defendant.
And if I refer to him as illegal.
And if I refer to him as a criminal.[4]

Metaphors make circles of our lives: a Venn diagram of contrast and resemblance.

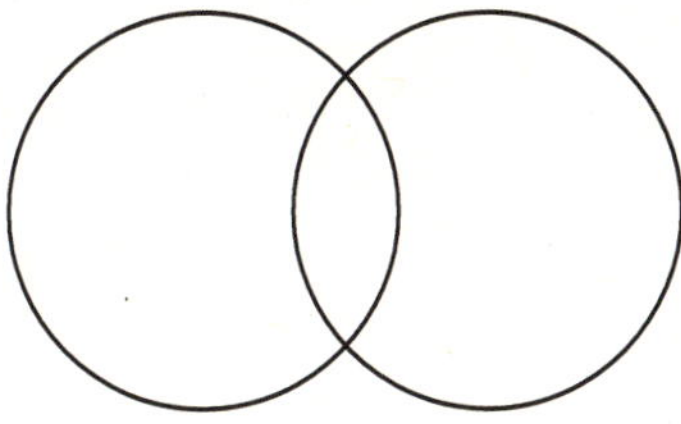

Who goes where?

8 In this year of social media algorithms, big data, fake news, alt-fact and news bot, documentary poetries offer a tradition and a space in which a writer can situate events or experiences within broader histories and fields of reference, without the burdens of mainstream journalism's anxiety over "balanced coverage," its obsession for presenting "both sides" to issues that are matters of fact, its imperative to build ratings or market share, its tendency toward representing opinions that favor middle-class white stability. (See NPR.)

Investigative or documentary poetry or prose can be a space to record, to unearth, and to help understand events as part of larger systems and legacies. But as poets and documentarians, we should not fetishize the document. In isolation it is meaningless, a blank slate upon which any story can be written. (See Wikileaks or Vanessa Place.)

The first step in extending the document might be to discern its limits and to situate it against other points of reference that expand its narrative, reveal its origins, and complicate its meaning.

Rukeyser knew this.

Sometimes we need to deface the documents to write back through them or into them, to fill in what's been left out or suppressed, to break a cage of words or reveal a cage of words in order to speak some version of a truth.

In the poem "West Virginia," Rukeyser transcribes an historic marker at the site of John Brown's execution ("Site of the Execution of John Brown Leader of the Raid at Harper's Ferry") then writes in between its language:

> the granite SITE OF THE precursor EXECUTION
> sabres, apostles, OF JOHN BROWN LEADER OF THE
> War's brilliant cloudy RAID AT HARPER'S FERRY

With her addition of "sabres, apostles" on the monument, Rukeyser makes Brown (whom she describes elsewhere as "that meteor") both activist and martyr. She does more than cite the official record, she responds to it.

9

Whereas Native Peoples are [ ] people with a deep and abiding [ ] in the [ ], and for millennia Native Peoples have maintained a powerful [ ] connection to this land, as evidenced by their [ ] and legends;

•

Whereas the Federal Government condemned the [ ], [ ], and [ ] of Native Peoples and endeavored to assimilate them by such policies as the redistribution of land under the Act of February 8, 1887 (25 U.S.C. 331; 24 Stat. 388, chapter 119) (commonly known as the "General Allotment Act"), and the forcible removal of Native [ ] from their [ ] to faraway boarding schools where their Native [ ] and [ ] were degraded and forbidden;

[spiritual]

[belief] [Creator]

[spiritual]

[customs]

[traditions]

[beliefs] [customs]

[children] [families]

[practices]

[languages]

10 When writing *Whereas,* Layli Long Soldier focused her attention on one official document, the congressional resolution of apology to Native Americans, which President Barack Obama signed in obscurity in 2009.

She divides her book into sections whose titles are borrowed from the apology: "These Being the Concerns," "Whereas Statements," "Resolutions," "Disclaimer." Throughout the book, she references the many ways in which the US government used language against Native Americans. "I've had difficulty unraveling the terms of these treaties, given the legal speak and congressional language," she explains in the poem "38" in which she recounts the execution of 38 Dakota men under orders from President Abraham Lincoln. These documents, she writes, are "a muddy, switchback trail to follow."

In another poem, she reproduces a section of the resolution from which she has removed a series of words. Many important books in the past few years have used redaction as a way to reveal the underlying logics and violence in official documents from trade agreements to military handbooks as well as to show the limits of such official language. Here I am thinking of works such as *Sand Opera* by Phillip Metres, *Anti-Humbolt* by Hugo García Manríquez and *Look* by Solmaz Sharif, among others. (In *Look,* for example, Sharif's erasures lay bare how casually the language of war is gendered or sexed.)

Long Soldier expands the project of erasure by reproducing the words that she initially removed ("spiritual," "belief," "Creator," "customs," and "traditions") within brackets on a subsequent page. She writes "...so I place/ a black bracket/ on either side of /an [idea] I cordon it/to safety away/from national re/solution the threat/ of re/ductive/ [thinking]." In an interview, Long Soldier explains: "I removed from that national document ....[its] hold on our spiritual life, our beliefs."[5] More than redaction, hers is a work of protection.

Like Rukeyser, poets must attempt to access the stories locked in the text or excluded from it. Like Long Soldier, we can draw attention to the ways in which official documents obscure the violence against our communities. We can make a poem a space to deface the monuments or reveal the brutality of the document or the violence it represents.

What documentary monument can you desecrate to bring flesh to story?

Can the poet extend the document like a blanket across the desert, can they shelter migrant men, women, and children from the gaze of the state?

Perhaps.

"The Desert Survival Series," created by the Electronic Disturbance Theater 2.0/b.a.n.g. lab, constitutes a long poem in 24 sections that provides lyric survival tools to assist migrants crossing the desert. The poem formed part of the Transborder Immigrant Tool, "a last mile safety device designed to aid the disoriented of any nationality in a desert environment."[6] The project included downloadable code meant to provide the coordinates of functional water caches, as well as poems (translated from English into Spanish and Arabic) that offered information to aid migrants trying to survive in a desert landscape. For example, one poem notes: "...if the barrel cactus — known otherwise as the compass cactus — stockpiles moisture; it also affords direction. As clear as an arrow or a constellation, it leans south."

"The Desert Survival Series" might offer an example of my preferred documentary: lyric and useful, observant and subversive, multilingual.

Poet, do you stand like the barrel cactus with your face full of sun or do you turn away?

As a citizen, consumer, stockholder, do we participate in the destruction of other economies, destabilize a society (through political intervention, the deportation of criminals, through criminal demand for illegal substances or cheap merchandise), then deny those who suffer most directly from our actions an opportunity to escape the conditions we create?

you understand the rights that you are giving up, the consequences of pleadin
ty and the terms of your written plea agreement?

11

voluntarily and of your own free will?
United States?
or about March 17, 2017 did you enter the United States from Mexico near Nogale
out coming through a designated port of entry?
v do you plead to the charge of illegal entry?
you understand the rights that you are giving up, the consequences of pleadin
ty and the terms of your written plea agreement? Are you pleading guilty voluntaril
of your own free will? Are you a citizen of the United States? On or about Marcl
2017 did you enter the United States from Mexico near Lukeville without comin
ugh a designated port of entry? How do you plead to the charge of illegal entry?
you understand the rights that you are giving up, the consequences of pleadin
ty and the terms of your written plea agreement? Are you pleading guilty voluntaril
you understand the rights that you are giving up, the consequences of pleading
of your own free will? Are you a citizen of the United States? On or about March 1
ilty and the terms of your written plea agreement? Ar
did you enter the United States from Mexico near Sasabe without coming throug
signated port of entry? How do you plead to the charge of illegal entry? Do yo

Illegal

Citizen

Understand

Illegal

Consequences

Citizen

Understand

Illegal

Citizen

Consequences

12 The word "economic" does not appear in the text of the Department of Homeland Security's webpage entitled "Obtaining Asylum in the United States." The word "family" is absent. The word "asylum" is only spoken into the record twice in reference to a legal privilege the court cannot grant.

A frame structures. An archive divides. The state often determines the terms that govern both. Suppressions abound, an old trick of white supremacy (ref: the Gag Rule, a series of rules that prevented any mention of slavery on the floor in the US House of Representatives from 1836-1844, by tabling, without discussion, any petitions that contained the word or Georgia Republican Rep. Doug Collins' recent accusation that Speaker Nancy Pelosi violated House rules on decorum when calling one of President Donald Trump's tweets racist.)

We must not replicate the elisions of the state. As poets and documentarians, we can extend the document or deface it to discern its limits and to situate it against those other sources that broaden its narrative, reveal its omissions, lay bare its brutality.

There is the court record, and then there are the articles of clothing found and four sets of remains recovered in five days in December 2016 from volunteers searching in the area near Ajo, Arizona.[7]

There is the court record and then there are the poems of Javier Zamora, a Salvadoran poet, who crossed the desert here near Tucson. He writes in the poem "Letter to the President Elect:"

> We craved water;
> our piss turned the brightest yellow—I am not the only nine-year-old
> that has slipped my backpack under the rancher's fences....

To access the stories erased, sometimes we must record the knowledge we receive from our unarchived experiences, look to folk tales, gossip, rumor, dream, the talk that talks like trees underground sharing sugar and water and energy, the talk we talk in poetry.

In her essay, "Poetry is not a Luxury," Audre Lorde writes: "For there are no new ideas. There are only new ways of making them felt... ."

To which I add this corollary: There may be no new atrocities, only the imperative to make them newly felt.

FOR FURTHER STUDY (DEAR MURIEL)

How can the poet stand as witness or court stenographer?

How can the poet change the course of the court proceedings—a bank of clouds pushing river to flood?

Can the poem be passport, naturalization certificate, social security card, be shield or gang or gun? Explain

How can the documentarian in a courthouse in the desert bring a flood?

NOTES: FRAMES, ERASURES, GRAFFITI

[1] In 2017, when I began writing this book, information about obtaining asylum could be found on the US Department of Homeland Security's webpage entitled "Obtaining Asylum in the United States." As I conclude this book in 2019, the page now simply entitled "Asylum," still does not mention the word "economic." There is, however, an alert on the top of the page referring to a recent US Citizenship and Immigration Services memorandum on procedures for "Unaccompanied Alien Children" that had been temporarily enjoined by court order.

In 2017, the 9th US Circuit Court of Appeals ruled the use of shackles in court violated detainees' right to the presumption of innocence before their cases were decided. For a time, the shackles were removed from detainees before entering the courtroom and replaced once they left. However, the Supreme Court ruled individual states had the right to mandate their use. In Arizona, migrants continue to be shackled.

Immigration policies have changed rapidly (and recklessly) during the Trump administration. The information presented in these pages represents the policies and realities that were in place and unfolding at the time of their writing.

[2] Many factors contribute to migration. Both economic conditions and violence in Mexico and Central America can be traced to decades of US policies. Among many sources see: Sayak Valencia's *Gore Capitalism* or Eduardo Galeano's *Century of the Wind*. Climate change has worsened many of these factors. For example, reporter Ryan Devereaux notes that in 2016: "the Food and Agriculture Organization of the United Nations reported that drought in Central America's dry corridor had left 3.5 million people **in need of humanitarian assistance**. USAID called it 'one of the worst droughts in 35 years in Central America.'" See Devereaux's "Mining the Future. Climate Change, Migration, and Militarization in Arizona's Borderlands," *The Intercept*, (Oct 3, 2019).

[3] Brady McCombs, "Crossing More Dangerous Than Ever for Migrants?" *Arizona Daily Star*, (August 4, 2011): web.

[4] While Trump may have coined the term "bad hombres" in reference to migrants coming through the US-Mexico border, the legacy of criminalizing black and brown bodies extends back to the founding of the United States. Scholar Jackie Wang notes that often innocence has become a precondition for inciting the sympathies of large protest movements that critique state sponsored violence against people of color. See *Carceral Capitalism*, Chapter 6, "Against Innocence."

[5] Layli Long Soldier, interview by Krista Tippett., *On Being*, SoundCloud, Oct 2018.

[6] Electronic Disturbance Theater 2.0/b.a.n.g. lab, *Transborder Immigrant Tool/ La herramienta transfronteriza para inmigrantes* (Ann Arbor, Michigan: The Office of Net Assessment, 2014), unnumbered acknowledgment page.

[7] Curt Prendergast, "Four sets of remains found in Ajo area in new effort on crossers," *Arizona Daily Star* (Dec 30, 2016). For a lyric account of such discoveries, see Margaree Little's *Rest*. For a visual representation of migrant deaths, see the work of the Tucson-based artist Alvaro Enciso, who has built and placed 900 crosses in the Sonora desert over the past five years to mark the sites where migrants' remains have been found. He calls his project "Where Dreams Die."

WRITING IN RELATION

13

Photos by GLENN KOENIG / Los Angeles Times

Sang P. Hong, one of 800 who became U.S. citizens Friday, reveled in "the spirit of this wonderful, happy day."

Citizen Gain

Uncertainty Over New Laws Sets Off a Rush to Naturalize

By LILY DIZON
TIMES STAFF WRITER

BUENA PARK—Many didn't know the words to the National Anthem, so they hummed. Loudly. Where they couldn't remember parts of the Pledge of Allegiance, they ad-libbed by mouthing words, any words.

So what if these newly sworn-in American citizens stumbled over parts of these well-known rites? "It is all in the heart," explained Sang P. Hong, placing her hands just there, "all in the spirit of this wonderful, happy day."

The 55-year-old Anaheim resident, of Korean descent, was one of 800 immigrants who took the Oath of Allegiance and became U.S. citizens Friday at an emotional ceremony at the Sequoia Athletic Club.

New citizen Teresa Rojas Peña is congratulated by her son Gonzalo Peña after the ceremony.

The ceremony marked the fourth time the Immigration and Naturalization Service performed the event in Orange County this year, the most the INS has ever had in the area in one year.

The pace reflected a trend: More and more immigrants are applying for U.S. citizenship. In past years, the INS performed only one or two ceremonies in Orange County, spokesman Rico Cabrera said.

INS officials attributed the increased number of applicants, in part, to the growing concerns stemming from anti-immigration sentiment and proposed policy such as Proposition 187, the state ballot initiative passed by voters last year that would eliminate most nonemergency public services for illegal immigrants.

A federal judge has ruled much of the law unconstitutional, but many people still believe their benefits may be cut, said Jane Arellano, an INS official in Los Angeles.

Cesar and Perigrina Ramirez of Peru said they have heard rumors of laws that would oust some immigrants from the United States. So, after 20 years of living as permanent residents here, the Santa Ana couple decided to become citizens, "just in case."

"We don't know what the laws are going to do and don't

Please see CITIZENS, B10

quez, 52, of Santa Ana, as she proudly waved her citizenship certificate. She and her husband, Alejandro, left Mexico 16 years ago.

"I always felt like I only worked here in this country," she said. "Now, I belong here."

The 800 naturalized citizens rep-

graded their computer system, Arellano said.

"We hope that by summer '96, we will only have an applicant waiting six months from the time of filing to oath-taking," instead of

Joanna Nachurski, 30, of Anaheim had tears in her eyes when she repeated the oath, administered by U.S. District Judge Gary L. Taylor. "It's still my country," she said of Poland. "I have so great feelings for

"I have to go on. This country has accepted me and it's time that I accept it as my new home," Nguyen said. "By roots, I am Vietnamese. But on paper, I am now an American."

Alien Registration No. 1283085

Name Anna (First name) (Middle name) Briante (Last name)

RIGHT
INDEX FINGERPRINT

Witness By
Louis Brian
20 [illegible]
Newark, N.J.

her
+
mark

Signature
of holder) Anna BRiaoti

16—26150—1

Birth date August 31 1880
(Month) (Day) (Year)

Born in or near Caposaco Avellino Italy
(City) (Province) (Country)

Citizen or subject of Italy
(Country)

Length of residence in United States 37 yrs., 3 mos.

Address of residence 51 Highland Ave
(Street address or rural route)

Newark Essex N.J.
(City) (County) (State)

Height 5 ft., — in.

Weight 190 lb.

Color of hair white

Distinctive marks none

(STAMP)

NEWARK, N.J.
FEB 17 1942
M.O.B.

Minna Groebel
(Signature of Identification Official)

Application filed in Alien Registration Division. Copy filed with Federal Bureau of Investigation office at

Newark N.J.

16—20150—1

14 In the final row of the courtroom, with a legal pad and a draft copy of the calendar, I can only glimpse the migrants' faces when they enter or exit. I lose track of which defendant speaks, can't hear what their lawyers say.

About Operation Streamline, **the poet Brandon Shimoda observes: "It is easy, in a space designed to bleed people of their stories, for the imagination to go dark and stay dark."**[8]

The court reporter's face is lit by a screen.
The marshal in the back row rubs his eyes, checks his phone.
Whatever I show you is a representation, filtered and partial.

"If poetry is an archive, then so too is a poem—or any text—and the writer is a kind of archivist..." writes poet and critic Joseph Harrington. "This issue [is] an especially important one for those who would include documents in poetry. Which documents? And why not include them all?"[9]

Just as the document elides and erases, so does the poem and the poet.

As witnesses, as researchers, as those who possess an "imagination enlarged by compassion," (to rewrite Shelley) we need to understand our documents as well as ourselves within the web of power and processes that produce them.

Sometimes it helps to sit inside a building and feverishly recreate what's beyond its walls, in order discern one's orientation.

As the poet Kristin Prevallet reminds us: "If poetry (or prose) for that matter is 'relational[,]' it is not because it appropriates sources as conquered territories, forcing them into the logic of the new text or subordinating them to some notion of perfection or 'totality.'"[10] Here she references Édouard Glissant's theories of relational poetics and continues: "Rather, Relational poetics looks at texts as being themselves in a constant state of motion, dispersion, and permeability that is inseparable not only from the shifting social and political context, but from the cycles of the earth and the diversity of nature."

We cannot use the documents to serve the "logic" of our poems or our world views, but we can use the poem to expand our view of the world. The reading or writing of a poem can help us to reflect on our place within the spheres of power and powerlessness that constitute our world.

Behind each name on each document: a face, a story, an opportunity for complication /connection. That will not be static; that can't be dependable.

15 I studied journalism as an undergraduate because I wanted to "give voice," as if a voice were anything to be "given." Faulty equations of:

Event/testimony + writer/witness = voice

I thought I could transform, word to word, I thought spark, I thought field on fire.

But eventually I began to wonder: Who walks that field with me? To whom does it belong? Whose voice can be heard over each step? The grasshoppers take to the air before my footfalls in waves, as if to make the prairie grass into water. How can I continue on my path without harming any potential you?

When James Agee went to the Alabama woods with photographer Walker Evans to document the lives of sharecroppers in the summer of 1936, he staggered and stumbled through his representations of the tenant families upon whose lives he was hired to report:

> I realize that, with even so much involvement in explanations as this, I am liable seriously, and perhaps irretrievably, to obscure what would at best be hard enough to give its appropriate clarity and intensity; and what seems to me most important of all: namely, that these I will write of are human beings, living in this world, innocent of such twistings as these which are taking place over their heads; and that they were dwelt among, investigated, spied on, revered and loved, by other quite monstrously alien human beings in the employment of still others, who have picked up their living as casually as if it were a book, and who were actuated toward this reading by various possible reflexes of sympathy, curiosity, idleness, et cetera, and almost certainly in a lack of consciousness, and conscience, remotely appropriate to the enormity of what they are doing.[11]

Agee deviates from many of his contemporaries by contemplating the conditions in which his documentary reporting was produced, as well as the situations in which it would be consumed. Though he does not always transcend his own privilege in his assumptions about his subjects (Are they really as naïve as he portrays them in their lack of knowledge of "such twistings" as those he describes as taking place over their heads?), he does offer a model for attempting to account for power imbalances inherent in the documentary project. In doing so, he ruptures the plane of objectivity, laying bare his perspective as partial and incomplete. In *Let Us Now Praise Famous Men,* he offers his ruminations, imaginings, misgivings, and meticulous depictions of the sharecroppers' existence. (He devotes 25 pages to describing the sharecroppers' clothing.) He lists his influences: William Blake, Jesus Christ, and Sigmund Freud, among others, under the heading "unpaid agitators." In doing so, he produces a wildly experimental, often lyrically stunning, sometimes infuriating, sometimes tender map of his inner struggles.

16 To look into the face of another is to skew late capitalism's calculations of "<" and ">."

To look into the face of another is the first step to filling in the ever-shifting map that charts our connections and complicity, the writing that reveals inequalities as well as joy and beauty (that is not always ours), as we place ourselves in relation, in love, in an ethics and activism.

Documents silence. One person's story can be used to erase another's. One person's narrative can do as much to uphold an imperialist white supremacist capitalist patriarchy as it can to dismantle it.

Be distrustful of a state that does not allow you to look
at the faces of the people it parades into a courtroom in chains.

Only in the turn to the other can we begin to grasp the simultaneity of presence: drone strikes in Pakistan, arsenic in our rice, ICE detention centers scattered like shrapnel throughout the United States. Beyond all document or testimony, to look into the face of another is to be open to particle and quark, verse and pollen, is to be open to change.

Systems monster. Data stories us.

And often what looks like safe passage, if not simply survival, is predicated upon making life more dangerous for others.

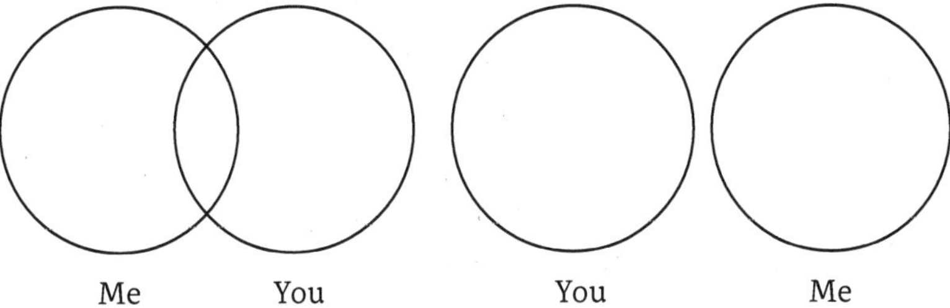

Can both be true in the many sourced versions of us?

17

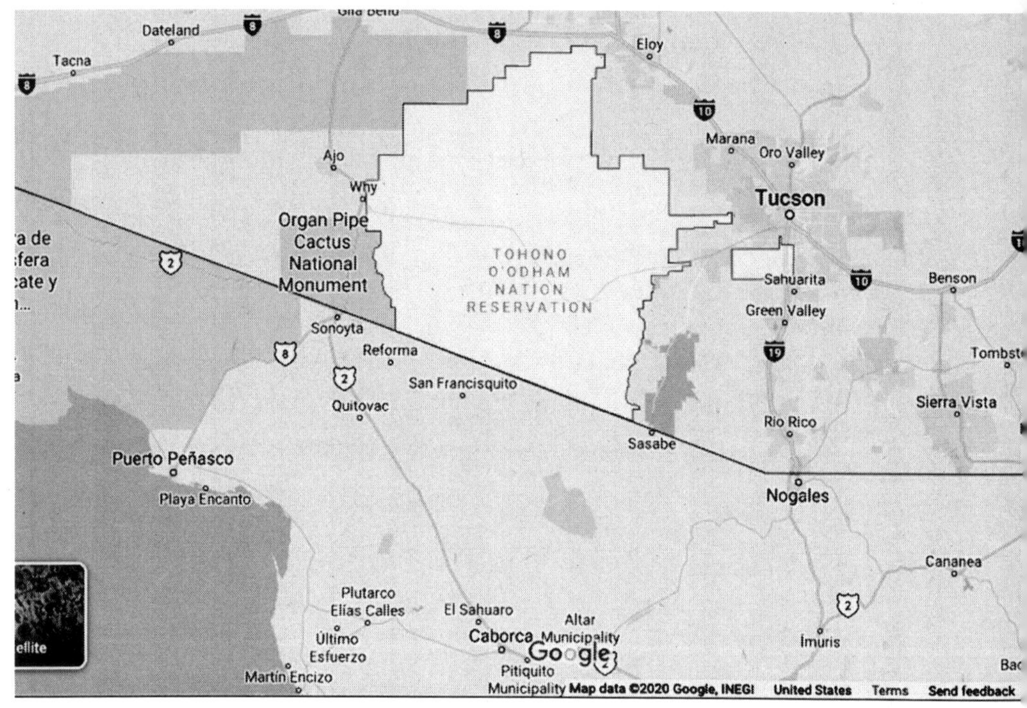

Dateland
Tacna
Eloy
Marana
Oro Valley
Ajo
Why
Tucson
Organ Pipe Cactus National Monument
TOHONO O'ODHAM NATION RESERVATION
Sahuarita
Benson
Green Valley
Sonoyta
Reforma
San Francisquito
Quitovac
Sierra Vista
Rio Rico
Sasabe
Puerto Peñasco
Playa Encanto
Nogales
Cananea
Plutarco Elías Calles
El Sahuaro
Altar
Último Esfuerzo
Caborca
Altar Municipality
Ímuris
Pitiquito Municipality
Martín Encizo
Google
Map data ©2020 Google, INEGI
United States
Terms
Send feedback

18 In a safe in our bedroom closet in our bank owned house, 72 miles from the US-Mexico border, on traditional lands of the Tohono O'odham Nation, my husband Farid keeps his naturalization certificate, a newspaper clipping of his naturalization ceremony, and a letter from then President Bill Clinton.

"I want to congratulate you on reaching the impressive milestone of becoming a citizen of our great nation..." President Clinton writes. "You now share in a great experiment: a nation dedicated to the ideal that all of us are created equal, a nation with profound respect for individual rights."

Not a "milestone," Farid calls his naturalization a "defensive measure" at a moment of heightened anti-immigration rhetoric from politicians such as Newt Gingrich, former Republican Speaker of the House of Representatives, and Pete Wilson, former governor of California where Farid and his family were living at the time.

The nation was founded on stolen lands.
An ideal is an abstract contract.
In an experiment, there is no certainty.

On my laptop, I open a scan of my great-grandmother's enemy alien identification card, issued in 1942, when she had been living in the United States for 37 years. The US government required the card be carried by Italian-born immigrants (classified as "enemy aliens") during World War II as part of a series of measures that included travel restrictions, the seizure of personal property, and internment. My great-grandmother signs her name on the card with an "X" beneath which are written the words "her mark," then "witnessed by" and the name and address of her son. Because of her illiteracy and the war with fascist Italy, she could be deported under the current president's immigration policy.

But she was not.

And although I live on occupied lands, nobody asks for my papers.

From my great-grandmother's illiteracy to my place in the middle class might seem a story of American opportunity, where generations appear like steppingstones toward some goal of a mortgage and a 401k. But the documents do not make evident the structures of white supremacy and limited economic expansion that made "progress" possible, what rights my ancestors' luck, effort, and assimilation have afforded me.

Metaphors make circles of our histories: a Venn diagram of contrast and resemblance.

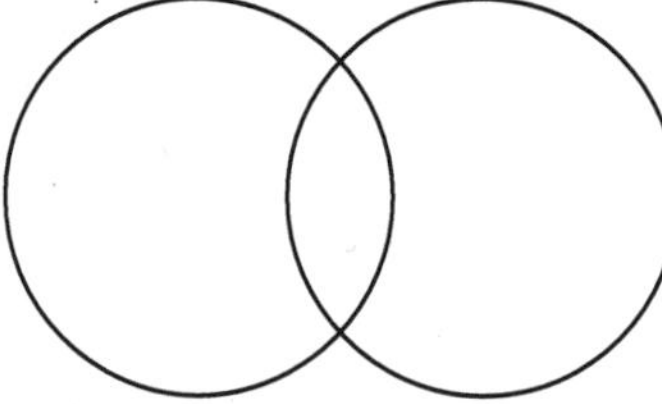

I do not want my family's story to be a frame, bent to resemble a human cage.

19 On the US side of the Nogales border, an unmarked white van parks just near the DeConcini border crossing. It is Summer 2017, and Mexican officials in brown uniforms greet the deportees, who step out of the van carrying large plastic "evidence" bags from the US Department of Homeland Security containing whatever they had on them when the Border Patrol or ICE agents wrenched them from their lives

in the Arizona desert or on the streets of Denver or San Francisco.

In Nogales, Sonora, at the Migrant Aid Center or *comedor* (dining hall), volunteers from the Kino Border Initiative provide free family-style meals to the men and women waiting to cross or who have crossed and have been deported here. They show a video from the Mexican Human Rights commission. "You have the right to work," the man in a broad cowboy hat from the video tells them. "You have the right to be with your family."

After the video, a nun tells the men to avoid the Nogales hotels, to avoid taking taxis, to stay at the shelter, to never borrow a phone from a stranger. Volunteers from the migrant rights group No More Deaths help the migrants cash the checks they received for the amount of money they carried in cash at the time of their arrest or apprehension. (And the carceral system makes money from their money.) A volunteer allows the migrants to use a phone to contact relatives.

There are clothes in the bathroom. There is a volunteer medic to provide first aid.

Black pins dot a desert map on the wall of the comedor to show where the bodies of migrants had been found. More than 3000 human remains have been found in Sonoran Desert, most of them migrants.[12]

A migrant tells me: "We just want to work."

When we ask how we can help, a volunteer at the *comedor* explains, "We need more shoes and backpacks."

20

CERTIFICATO di NASCITA e BATTESIMO

Chiesa di Santa Lucia

Newark, New Jersey,

STATI UNITI D'AMERICA.

Con Questo si Certifica che

Gerardo Brianti

figlio di Alfonso e

di Anna Ceres nacque

il giorno 18 del mese Settembre 1904 e fu

battezzato il giorno 13 del mese Dicembre 1904

dal Rev. Antonio De Falco

Padrini: { Nicola Malanga
Angela Maria Tobia

per Il Parroco

Rev. V. Cuccaro

Per copia conforme

In fede, Newark, N. J. 13 Dicembre 1904

21 In the first decade of the last century when my great-grandfather emigrated from Italy to the United States through New Orleans, he did not carry a passport.

We do not know why he did not stay in New Orleans, but in 1891, eleven Italian-Americans were lynched in that city, a strange hinge in a history of assimilation and racism that swings around me. My great-grandfather eventually settled in Newark, NJ, where he worked as a mason on the building of the Basilica of the Sacred Heart. On the 1920 census, his occupation is listed as "construction."

What color was he when he walked off the boat?

An average of 200,000 Italians entered the United States each year in the first decade of the 20th century, three of my great grandfathers among them.

By 1920, many governments begin to adopt the worldwide passport standard championed by the League of Nations. One year later, the United States Congress passed the Emergency Quota Act restricting the number of immigrants from certain countries, including Italy, who were now easily identifiable. Then Congress passed the even more restrictive Immigration Act of 1924, which initially imposed a total quota on immigration for countries outside the Western Hemisphere of 165,000—less than 20 percent of the pre-World War I average—placing the most restrictive quotas on immigrants from countries that were deemed *less desirable*. With the 1924 Act, the annual quota for Italians was set at less than 4,000.

During congressional debate over the 1924 Act, Senator Ellison DuRant Smith of South Carolina explained: "I think that we have sufficient stock in America now for us to shut the door, Americanize what we have, and save the resources of America for the natural increase of our population."

"Who is an American?" the senator continued, "Is he an immigrant from Italy? Is he an immigrant from Germany? If you were to go abroad and someone were to meet you and say, 'I met a typical American,' what would flash into your mind as a typical American, the typical representative of that new Nation? Would it be the son of an Italian immigrant, the son of a German immigrant, the son of any of the breeds from the Orient, the son of the denizens of Africa?"

The quota system remained in effect until 1965. And in between: the internment of Japanese Americans and to a lesser degree the internment of Italian Americans, the Jim Crow reign of terror, the lynching of African Americans, Mexican Americans and other people of color, the Bracero program, the beginning of the Civil Rights movement, the tragedy of American Indian residential schools. By the 1940s, popular representations of American identity offered protagonists with English sounding names and a physical Nordicism. As historian Nell Irvin Painter explains: "With real American identity coded according to race, being a real American often meant joining antiblack racism, and seeing oneself as white against the blacks."[13]

In the first decade of the last century, when he emigrated from Italy to the United States through New Orleans, could he have known what he was bringing us into?

Among our family myths: a story about him watching his grandchildren walk to school with "tears in his eyes." Perhaps those tears suggest his pride at his grandchildren speaking English or going to school. Perhaps those tears reflect what was lost. In either case, immigration quotas, as well as racism and ethnocentrism, helped to police linguistic and cultural assimilation allowing some ethnicities access to "whiteness" as adopted cultural norms including the practice of racism, what Senator Durant Smith called the process of "Americanization."

Among the family documents: my great uncle's baptism certificate from St Lucy's Church in Newark, NJ from 1904 written entirely in Italian, a language which no one in the family speaks anymore.

Citizenship has a price.

Who pays the debt?

"Citizenship is a recursive performance," Brandon Shimoda says.[14]

The past is a text in which some sentences are redacted while others change. I read it in relation

to understand my place in history as my place in capitalism's supply chain.

Who sits on the bench and cries for what?

Citizenship is a construct, a shelter that was never constructed to cover everyone equally, that may never have been constructed to cover everyone.

Most of the stories of my three great-grandfathers from Italy drowned across the whispers and repressions of a family as if an ocean. My mother's father would drink himself to rag. No one mentions the small rooms, the rage. No one chooses to tell that story.

We have no documents to show my great-grandparents ever became citizens.

Today, according to the UN Refugee Agency, 10 million people around the world are stateless.

22 In the fifth-floor apartment that serves as a migrant women and children's shelter in Nogales, Sonora: an 18-year-old girl who wants to see her father, a woman from Central America who left under death threat, a mother who fled an abusive relationship and now needs to make more money to support her children and grandchildren, and an 80-year-old who wants to cross into Nogales, AZ, for the eighth time so she can sell *paletas* from a pushcart.

A nun prods them into telling their stories to us: four women and one man visiting from a creative writing program at a state university just an hour north of them through an initiative that aims to use literary and documentary arts to diversify the stories about and expand dialogue on issues related to the border.[15]

The eldest woman stands raising her hand as if testifying or praying. She says when the first President Bush came into office, he tried to make life hard for migrants. But we rose up, she explains, and stopped him. She says as soon as she can, she will go back to the popsicle factory, to her boss. She tells us her boss's name and address, says her boss will give her a card to help her stay

as soon as she can get back.

And the woman who fled her country under death threat says: "We want peace." Decades of US policies and interventions in Central America that favor business interests over the majority of the population, that export gang members and failed anti-gang policies, must feel like a long, dirty war.

"Do you feel better when you tell these stories?" one of us asks. And the woman does not answer, just keeps telling her story.

"We are teaching them to make earrings," the nun explains as she brings us into another room and shows us beaded jewelry: row upon row, each piece a little memorial to every woman who has come through the shelter.

What did the nun tell them about our presence or what we might be able to do for them? Were they told we could help? Were they told we could help before the end of their two-week stay at the woman's shelter after which they would have to find their way north or back from where they came? Were they told some faulty equation of voice and change, some scrawl of hope like the flight of sparrows, stalling and diving without knowing whose house they alight upon?

What did we think we could do? Every summer for the past three I have gone to Nogales, Mexico, with students from the University of Arizona's MFA in Creative Writing Southwest Field Studies in Writing Program to witness and write about migration and environment issues unique to southern Arizona. And each summer, as we bear witness to conditions migrants face, we wonder: **How can we amplify voices without turning other people's stories into commodities, without re-affirming the faulty myth of "giving voice"?** We do not want to reduce the struggles of the migrants we meet to mere human-interest stories. We know that writing will not be enough.

The change necessary to improve the migrant women's lives feels utterly available and beyond any single transaction.

"We will work hard," the women tell us.

"Do you have bracelets?" we eventually ask.

23 I sit on my living room couch with my laptop, working through cartographies of relation while monsoon clouds gather south of me.

Upon which scale should I plot the distance between me and Anna Ceres Brianti, a little blood and silence, a little blood and a line of cause and effect, an artery of conditions without which I would not be here?

Upon which scale should I plot the distance between me and the men and women who stood before the judge in shackles? Between me and four women who sat on the couch in the Nogales apartment?

A line of cause of effect that stretches from me to the border

where I have not yet gone to burn my passport in protest.

Is this my story when I become your great-granddaughter?

Is this my story when I become your witness?

Is this my story when the political and economic policies of my country and the corporations I feed (with every necessary or unnecessary purchase) cause your poverty or export their violence?

24 In the aftermath of Hurricane Katrina, poet and New Orleans native Abe Louise Young began a project of transcribing the oral histories of the victims of the storm and of government policy failures. Young archived the project on the website *Alive in Truth: the New Orleans Disaster Oral History Project.* About the work, Young writes:

> When I launched *Alive in Truth: The New Orleans Disaster Oral History and Memory Project* in the week after Hurricane Katrina hit, my goal was to help restore authorship and narrative control to people who had been assaulted by media images of themselves as criminals. I had a vague idea that one day I might work these testimonies into a book of poetry...but that notion was quickly discarded, in part because none of the narrators liked it. Rightfully, they wanted to be the authors, and they wanted their narratives published in full.[16]

Young continues to recount how the words of those narratives did find their way into a book, *Saltwater Empire*. Its author, Raymond McDaniel, used the personal histories of six African American Katrina survivors culled from the *Alive in Truth* website as "found poetry," collaged and stripped of attribution and context, to create his book's centerpiece poem. He did so without contacting Young or the survivors whose words he used.[17]

Young explains: "By neglecting to inquire, much less make certain that his plans were acceptable to the narrators, McDaniel reenacted a familiar racist pattern, and a blind spot in American poetry publishing was revealed...When a white person takes the voices of people of color for his own uses, without permission, in the aftermath of a racially charged national disaster, it is vulture work—worse than ventriloquism."[18]

There is more information, more data available to the poet than ever before. In this swarm of uncontextualized information, we need to ask the questions: Who controls and who sees such data? Whose stories are privileged and whose are silenced? What narratives are being made up about us?

Big data helps the traders on Wall Street make money algorithmically between the seconds across the date lines. But somewhere, too, scientists use big data to look for the "god" particle.

Like the physicist, the poet can turn to data to find the most elemental information about themselves and their world, tracing the intersections between individuals and systems, charting our connections and complicities, attuned to easy narratives set like traps, as well as the stories erased or unrecorded in all of this monitoring.

The poet should not NSA, collecting isolated data extracted from multiple frames of reference,[19] but the poet can train their sights to read their environment from multiple perspectives, opening the viewfinder with an awareness of larger landscapes.

My friend, the essayist and poet Metta Sáma, once wrote me: "I like to remember that writing is not just committing words to paper. It's committing the self to reflection, to percolation, to observing, to witnessing, to taking in, to dissecting, to organizing, to assessing, to synthesizing."[20]

Poet, do you make poems out of the suffering of others without considering how you are implicated in that suffering?

White poet, do you make poems out of the suffering of brown or black bodies without considering how you are implicated in that suffering?

Faced with a document do you wonder: whose story is this?

25 I know writers who will not write about the migrants they visit at the Eloy detention center. I know writers who save any money they make from writing about immigration issues to give to the migrants they visit at the Florence detention center. I know writers who struggle with whether or not they should write about the migrants they visit. The writer Raquel Gutiérrez asks about a not too different context: "Do you think they will write about themselves?"[21]

When I say we need to understand our documents as well as ourselves within the web of power and processes that produce them,

I do not mean I can speak for the migrant women in the shelter no matter how much I feel for them. I do not mean I get to imagine my way into their stories. I mean my compassion must compel me to see the ways directly or indirectly that I am implicated in their suffering.

In the early pages of *Let Us Now Praise Famous Men*, Agee describes a moment when he and photographer Walker Evans come across a locked church in the Alabama woods and want to be let inside to photograph it. As an African American man and woman walk past, Agee decides he will go after them to ask if they know someone who might be able to let him and Evans into the church. Agee describes what happens as he approaches them running from behind:

> At the sound of the twist of my shoe in the gravel, the young woman's whole body was jerked down tight as a fist into a crouch from which immediately, the rear foot skidding in the loose stone so that she nearly fell, like a kicked cow scrambling out of a creek eyes crazy, chin stretched tight, she sprang forward into the first motions of running...shaking my head and raising my palm outward, I came up to them (not trotting) and stopped a yard short of where they, closely, not touching now, stood and said, still shaking my head (No; no; oh Jesus, no, no, no!) and looking into their eyes at the man, who was not knowing what to do, and at the girl, whose eyes were lined with tears...[22]

In a moment in the Alabama woods it is as if all the weight and pain, the legacy of slavery and the systemic racism of the Jim Crow south, clamp down around them determinately in ways that Agee fails to predict or discern until he witnesses it. He continues:

> ...I could not bear that they should receive from me any added reflection of the shattering of their grace and dignity, and of the nakedness and depth and meaning of the fear, and of my horror and pity and self-hatred... "I'm very sorry! I'm very sorry if I scared you! I didn't mean to scare you at all. I wouldn't have done any such thing for anything."

Despite his intentions, Agee confronts what scholar Saidiya Hartman calls the inescapable "violence that animates this encounter."[23] Even in his moment of witnessing such violence, he does not transcend it: he compares the woman to an animal. And yet in Agee's awkward realization of that violence, in his stammering (*No; no; oh Jesus, no, no, no!)* Hartman hears something that might signal whiteness being made aware of itself and desirous to be something else:

> What distinguishes this moment is the artist's willingness to admit and to own the violence of the encounter. We might consider if this refusal to disavow the violence that is whiteness here in its benevolence and generosity, is a moment when whiteness itself trembles, yearns to oppose itself, when it invites its destruction, when it welcomes the dispossessive force that would make it just human, just animate, just life.

Any of us who write from positions of privilege (especially as those of us who are white) need to cultivate our ability to recognize the violence that our positions enact even unwittingly. We need to learn the violence carried and encoded upon our bodies. And instead of waiting to be confronted

we need to learn to seek that self-reflective and self-destructive trembling.

26 Our capacity to witness has increased at a disproportionate rate in relation to our ability to effect change. We can be lulled into a false sense of "activism" in our documenting the pain of others as easily as we can by reposting or retweeting every injustice we read.

"In an era when eyewitness testimonies, photos, and videos are tweeted seconds after a catastrophe, poetry's power to witness now feels outdated and inherently passive," writes Cathy Park Hong on the *Poetry Foundation* website. "But perhaps I feel this way since I am writing this when witness feels more powerless than ever. There were sixty-four witnesses when the grand jury reviewed the murder of Michael Brown, yet the grand jury failed to indict police officer Darren Wilson."

"It is not enough for the poem to be witness, to preserve a dated moment and give voice to puppets from the past," Hong explains. Instead she champions an art that unsettles, that evokes, that recognizes distance. "The proximity between you and me is infinite..." she writes. "I can never metabolize what you went through, yet I cannot escape your disquieting sadness, the burden of your solitude."

Hong refers to an art that refuses to NSA or surveil. It does not take dictation like a court reporter for the state. This is art wrought from a willingness to see beyond the margins of the document, beyond the people who stand before the judge in chains, beyond the gates and fences of the detention center, beyond the human cage.

27 My first-generation grandfather attended school until the eighth grade. During the depression, he dug graves. He "collected money." He worked as a laborer, lived on the bottom floor of a house owned by his brother (also a laborer). Until the day he died he could not leave a restaurant without taking packets of sugar, because he remembered when sugar was a commodity few could afford.

But his brother purchased his house in a neighborhood where other immigrants could not because of redlining practices. My grandfather benefited from opportunities that would have been denied an African American person. He was able to retire and drive across the country with his wife in his Chevy Impala without fear of being turned away at any hotel.

Because whiteness dawned upon him and his descendants like a sun or a bomb. To look at the histories of our families, of our nation, to see them for what they really are, beyond all rhetoric, would be to literally change history.

Dear documentarian, dear poet, what is the value
of your privilege?

In the classroom, my first-generation or second-generation immigrant students write their way through the traumas as well as the beauty of their experiences. They testify at the seminar table or on the page, they question, they challenge, they love, they fail, they rewire, they recalibrate, they remake the lyric.

Dear documentarian, dear poet, what will you renovate?

28 The words "economic," "family," and "asylum" remain unspoken as I sit in the back of the courtroom scribbling on a legal pad, trying to structure a context and trace my relation to the seven men who stand before the judge shackled at the wrists, waists, and ankles.

Reader, can you improvise your relation to the phrase "illegal entry," to the large seal of US District Court, District of Arizona, that hangs above the judge, eagle suspended with talons and arrows pointing?

Perhaps your relation stretches like a wall, bends like footprints towards a road, perhaps your relation spindles and barbs, chollas or ocotillos, twists like a razor wire on top of a fence.

Perhaps you do not improvise, perhaps you shackle, you type, you translate, you prosecute, you daily wage, your mouth goes dry when you speak—paper, palimpsests of silence, palimpsests of complicity and connection never made evident on the page.

Write down everything you need. How long is the list?
Sleep with it beneath your head, eat it, wear it.
Can you use it to make a little shade from an unrelenting gaze?

Speak into the court record the amount of profit extracted from such men as those before the judge shackled at the wrists, waists, and ankles not limited to the amount of profit that will be extracted from such bodies through the payments that will be made per prisoner per day to the Corrections Corporation of America and GEO Group, but also inclusive of all the profits generated by trade agreements that makes labor in the so-called developing countries so cheap.

How can we digest it?

"Best of luck to you," the judge says.

"Que le vaya bien," the lawyers say as the migrants[24] begin their slow procession out of the courtroom in chains.

And in that moment, from the back of the courtroom,
we can decide to accept or forget what we have seen, to bear it,
or to change it

because we love it, we want it, we don't care enough to stop it,
we hate it,

we can't imagine how to stop it, we can't imagine it,
we can't imagine.

FOR FURTHER STUDY (BEFORE THE DOCUMENTS OF THE STATE)

Does your name become a seed in the mouth of the document? What grows from it?

Does your name make a town? Have you seen it? Can you describe it?

Who authored its first misspelling? What would you tell them if you could?

Can the documentarian ask themself: who do you look to or like or for? Describe them.

NOTES: WRITING IN RELATION

[8] Brandon Shimoda, "Operation Streamline," *The New Inquiry*, (May 3, 2017): web.

[9] Joseph Harrington,"Docupoetry and Archive Desire," *Jacket2*, (October 27, 2011): web.

[10] Kristin Prevallet, "Writing is Never by Itself Alone: Six Mini-Essays on Relational Investigative Poetics," *Fence*, (Spring 2003): 20.

[11] James Agee and Walker Evans, *Let Us Now Praise Famous Men*, (Boston: Mariner Books, 2001), 10.

[12] See the Arizona OpenGIS Initiative for Deceased Migrants available through the Humane Borders website.

[13] Nell Irvin Painter, *The History of White People*, (New York: W.W. Norton & Co., 2011), 363.

[14] Brandon Shimoda and Farid Matuk in conversation, March 11, 2018, Tucson Festival of Books.

[15] Since the summer of 2017, I have codirected the University of Arizona's MFA in Creative Writing Southwest Field Studies in Writing Program. The program sends MFA students to write and research in residency for two weeks on the US-Mexico border. As part of the program, the students also offer creative writing workshops to marginalized youth and partner with community based social justice and environmental organizations. As of this writing, the program is on hiatus because of a lack of funding.

[16] Abe Louise Young, "The Voices of Hurricane Katrina, Part I." *Poetry Foundation* website, (Aug 18, 2010).

[17] McDaniel in an accompanying essay on the *Poetry Foundation* website explains that he tried to make evident the multiplicities of voices, including his own, in the work: "No reader could believe this voice was singular, even if it spoke as such, even as I tried to make the transitions as seamless as possible. I hoped this would both ease and confuse the reader's expectations of what it might mean to speak and be heard..."

He concludes: "Does it matter that I wanted to draw attention to a dangerously simplistic representation by making a more complex one if my methods cause offense? What if they offend some but compel others? No programmatic belief regarding what does or does not constitute appropriation, or what it even means, can adequately address all subsequent questions."

The *Alive in Truth: the New Orleans Disaster Oral History Project* website no longer exists.

[18] *Saltwater Empire* offers just one example of the kind of "ventriloquism." I offer it here because Young and McDaniel's essays on the *Poetry Foundation* website provide additional context for the book. This kind of vulture work can be seen in the poetries of Kenneth Goldsmith and Vanessa Place, who used documentary evidence of violence perpetrated on brown and black bodies, without context or consideration of the source. When Kenneth Goldsmith read the autopsy of Michael Brown in front of an audience at Brown University, he treated the document with a kind of impunity, with the logic of colonizer. Perhaps if he had sought permission of the Michael Brown's family and chose to read the autopsy in front of the Ferguson city council or the US Congress, the act would have had a different resonance. But he did not.

[19] We live at a time when every log-in and every purchase made, as well as each text, email, or photo sent, becomes tangled in a very large net formed by ubiquitous information-sensing mobile devices, aerial sensory technologies, software logs, cameras, microphones, and radio-frequency identification r eaders. A ll o f t his i s s tockpiled b y governments and corporations, a swirling fog of data.

[20] Metta Sáma, email message to author, July 16, 2019.

[21] Marianna Ariel shared with me this quote from Raquel Gutiérrez through an email exchange. When I asked Gutiérrez about it, she said she couldn't remember if she had written the question or posed it conversationally. She did approve of its use here. Sometimes when the trail of the document goes cold, your voice might carry far enough to get an answer to your questions.

[22] Agee and Evans, 38.

[23] Saidiya Hartman. "Near a Church at Dusk." (presentation, On Whiteness: A Symposium, June 2017): web.

[24] And you beyond this page, could you feel the country change beneath you? /Let the absence of your voice on the page stain the page/ to show the cracks/to be weedy/ the many footprints, the many sourced documents of you.

GUIDESTARS, TANGLES, HAUNTOLOGIES

HUMANE
FRONTERAS
Maestro Mauricio
Water
December

BORDERS
OMPASIVAS
Farah Gebara
tation
18, 2008

I.

Two hours either side of noon, insert a stick (one meter long) into the ground.

Mark the tip of the shadow it casts with a stone.

Wait twenty minutes.

Mark its second shadow with another stone.

Draw a straight line from the first stone to the second, extending the line two additional meters. This is your west to east axis.

Draw a perpendicular line that crosses its center.

Stand at the lines' intersection. Keep west to your left to face true north.

Pick a visible landmark in line with that orientation.

Walk to that landmark; repeat this exercise.

II.

At night, look for the Big Dipper.

Note the two stars that form its outer edge.

Imagine a line from those stars to a point about five times the distance between them. You should find Polaris, the North Star, waiting for you there (the end of the Little Dipper's handle).

Imagine a straight line between Polaris and the horizon. This is your second true north bearing.

30 The sign marking the Maestro Mauricio Farah Gebara Water Station for migrants (established and maintained by the nonprofit Humane Borders) shows the Big Dipper overflowing with water, acts as guide star for those migrants who might find it in the desert of southern Arizona. Pockmarked with bullet holes, adorned by a single string of plastic rosary beads, the sign serves as notice and map, art and orientation.

"What would I want from a poem in the desert?" writes Amy Sara Caroll, author of the "The Desert Survival Series." "Would I want a poem there at all?"[25] Caroll's poems were meant to be shared with migrants via the Transborder Immigrant Tool, a mobile phone app that would provide GPS coordinates to guide migrants to water stations as they made their way "to the United States through the deserts of the US/Mexico borderlands." So Caroll wrote poems to aid in the "emotional and mental well-being" of migrants as well as provide information on how to withstand a variety of desert conditions. She crafted the work using information gleaned by migrant aid organizations.[26] The poems (that would appear in Spanish, English, and Arabic) became data, became document in and of themselves in the warnings and support they provided their readers:

> In a sand or dust storm, heat suffocates; winds transubstantiate the landscape into unidentified flying objects. Sand becomes sandpaper against the skin. Turn your back to the wind. Lie on your side against a hill or dune. Wrap your face. Cover your nose and mouth. Tuck your eyeglasses into your shirt or jacket pocket (so the wind will not etch its soliloquies into them). Wait it out. No Godot, a sandstorm will go the way of a temper tantrum.[27]

Legal threats to the lab that created the Transborder Immigrant Tool and concerns around drug cartels' increased control of migration routes prevented the app's distribution. Still the poems and the code remain: vibrational waves of art/information released upon the world, sending their signals (of help as well as defiance) like the torn blue flag rising above the Maestro Mauricio Farah Gebara Water Station, about which poet and essayist Raquel Gutiérrez wrote: "I pledge allegiance to *this* flag."[28]

I want those poems and that code, that flag and the sign at the Maestro Mauricio Farah Gebara Water Station to serve as models for our documentary work at a time when the Pima County Medical examiner reports 127 remains were recovered in southern Arizona in 2018, when an Arizona court decided leaving gallons of water and cans of beans in a desert is a crime.

**Can the poem be a flag
to signal the presence of water?**

**Can a poem counter the violence
of the state?**

**Can the poem be a flag
staked like a claim to the future?**

31 On a sidewalk next to ivy, a poet lays down somewhere between Balmoral Ave and Landsbury Drive in the West London town of Hayes near the site of a 1979 race riot. On a service road in South Delhi, the poet lays down where a woman died after being raped "then thrown from a bus." The poet makes monuments, memorials, rituals, shrines, and protests. The poet forges alternate modes of perception gleaned from placing her head against the asphalt or soil to record colors and textures.[29]

In *Ban en banlieue*, Bhanu Kapil produces a series of notes to a novel never written about a gesture (a body? a corpse?), about a girl lying down on the sidewalk at some distance from a race riot, about the body of a girl thrown from a bus. In unrelenting and searing defamiliarizations, in color saturated descriptions, Kapil writes as if slipping a filter over our viewfinders or pulling it away ("Each cell gives off a tiny bit of light.") documenting with methodologies both imaginative and ethical.

"How can the body perform something in a new way," Kapil writes "something that belongs neither to the scene nor to history?"[30]

When Brenda Coultas writes about her New York City neighborhood in "The Bowery Project" poems from *A Handmade Museum*, she documents her surroundings as well as her own experiments and interactions, becoming both an actor and observer among the debris of her environs: dumpster diving, collecting stories from passersby on the street, giving tours of her and her husband's tenement. The titles of her poems suggest her methodology: "An Experiment in Misery," "Bowery Box of Wishes," "Things I Found December 15, 2001," "Sightings," and "A Summary of a Public Experiment."

Despite these attempts, Coultas's ultimate gesture marks the distance between herself and the transient men and women, who slept on the precarious streets of her neighborhood. In the poem, "A Summary of a Public Experiment," Coultas writes: "My own tale is of walking and observing, of imagining." And when she writes: "I was not a homeless or passed out on the sidewalk...." she reminds us: imaginings have limits.

The poet or documentarian can see beyond the frames of the scene influenced but not bound by history. The poet or documentarian might record obsessively (like Agee) or create the conditions to register new sensory data through performance, experiment, or exercise.

In their (Soma)tic poetry and poetics, CA Conrad creates rituals to thwart the "factory" of poetry production[31] and to place themselves within "an extreme present," to find a "new way of living," not just a new way of creating poetry. For example, in the ritual "Security Camera and Flowers Dreaming the Elevation Allegiance," Conrad, carrying a basket of edible flowers, stopped at every security camera on a single Philadelphia block, looked directly into each lens, stuck their tongue inside a flower and proclaimed: "I'm a pollinator, I'm a pollinator." This ritual generated new perspectives, performance, play, and protest, eventually resulting in a poem "I Want to do Every/ Thing Wrong Just Once," which includes the lines "suddenly we are/ a daisy under/ the big wheel" and "you think I'm afraid / of course I am/ I'm disgusted chopping us in two," perhaps alluding to interspecies understanding. Conrad describes the basics of (Soma) tics as a salve against capitalism's drain on individual and collective creativity.[32]

In performance, experiment and (Soma)tics, the poet or documentarian writes relationally, recording through and from the body, from their own subjectivities and presence. Such experiential research can be as somber as an unmarked tomb in the desert or as playful as sticking out a tongue at a security camera, can strengthen by its failure, must be relational and aware of the distances between experiences as it takes upon itself monumental tasks, makes of itself monuments or maps. Kapil writes:

> Body outline on ground ringed by candles/flowers ... The anti-rape protesters make a circle around my body when I lie down. What do they receive? An image. But what happens next? How does the energy of a performance mix with the energy of the memorial? How does the image support the work that is being done in other areas? Which hormones does it produce?
> —New Delhi, India, 2014

The silhouette of a body near the side of the road in West London or South Delhi might demarcate the necessary limits or failing of our sympathies. ("I can never metabolize what you went through," writes Cathy Park Hong.) The poet responds with questions opening new fields of inquiry and participation in the text. In experimenting with other (literal) points of view, looking up from the ground or into a camera, the poet documents the borders of subjectivity. The poet minds the edges of what Édouard Glissant calls an opacity or the right to more than "difference," the right to "subsistence within an irreducible singularity."[33]

But a shadow or a silhouette also marks the point where we might be moved to an action born out of compassion. Because it is not empathy that helps us as writers, as citizens, especially as those who occupy positions that have been privileged, when we write about what we can or cannot "imagine." Rather compassion or solidarity leads to action regardless of our ability to identify with those who suffer, makes us aware and respectful of difference. To learn from opacity is to learn from what we do not know, is to learn without mastery. Glissant reminds us that opacity "can make me sensitive to the limits of every method, it relativizes every possibility of every action within me."

Poets and documentarians can relativize their actions within a web of relations, to make the poem more than a receptacle of information forced into their already existing logics or realms of experience. Instead, the poem might be the catalyst for the production of sensory and affective data that explores and complicates those relations.

A poem can be an experiment or a tool or an occasion to call together the antirape protesters as well as to bring the words of laborers to the page. (See Mark Nowak and the Worker Writers School as well as the history of activist workshops he writes about in "Panthers, Patriots, and Poetries" and the book *Social Poetics*.[34]) The word "poem" comes from the Ancient Greek *poiesis* "the activity in which a person brings something into being that did not exist before," a making.

Amy Sara Caroll walked the desert before she wrote her poems.

Our documentary imperatives might move us off the page, eschewing unattainable goals of objectivity, a form fueled by hegemonic ways of seeing, a point of view that assumes our perceptions can be trusted and legible when removed from historical or individual context. Instead our documentary impulses might move us to provide experiential points of reference in our writing as well as opportunities to create tools for survival or for self and communal inquiry.

Venn diagrams make an eclipse, the beginning of an opacity, a shadow thrown between us:

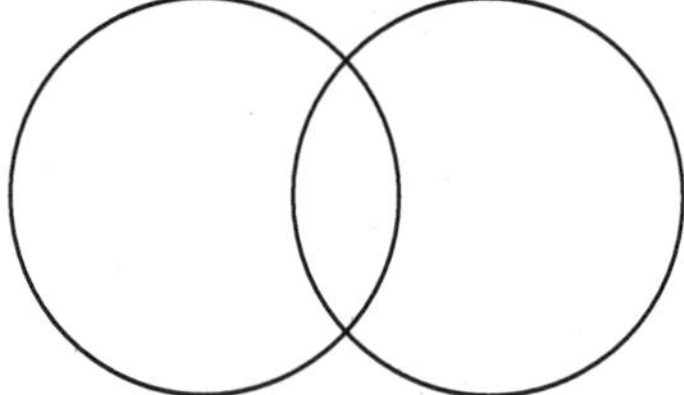

from which we might discern our relations.

32 In July 2018, before the DeConcini port of entry, 15 men, women, and children, who should not have to wait to be processed for asylum, wait to be processed for asylum sitting or lying on the sidewalk with makeshift beds and bags around them.

Their bodies on the ground are not performance, are an act of concrete under flesh sacrifice, are subjected to the sanctioned rituals of the state.

And if I lay my white woman's body on the border between Nogales, Arizona, and Nogales, Sonora, I do not become migrant although I might feel the pinch and pressure of cement under my hips, might smell how the concrete carries the odor of sun and piss. If I lay my white woman's body on the border between Nogales, Arizona, and Nogales, Sonora, my color changes the frame. My body reverberates against a different archive. For centuries a white woman's discomforts, tears, and accusations could be used to justify the disciplining, even death, of nonwhite bodies. My white woman's body draws or deflects attention in often violent ways.

In July 2019, I sit my body down on the sidewalk outside of the Kino Border Initiative's Migrant Aid Center with notebooks, coloring books, and crayons. A small group of children have followed me outside after the four o'clock meal.

Once single migrant men on their way to the United States or recently deported filled the *comedor*'s tables, now men, women, and children line up for the meal. Instead of watching a video before they eat, Sister Cecilia Lopez Arias leads them in a song: "*En el arca de Noé, todos caben, todos caben. En el arca de Noé, todos caben y yo también*." (In Noah's Ark, there's room for everyone. In Noah's Ark, there's room for everyone—including me.) In May 2018, as the Trump administration's turnback policy left increasing numbers of asylum seekers stuck in Nogales for weeks or months before they could present themselves to US Customs and Border Protection agents, the *comedor*'s tables began to fill with families. Many of the men, women, and children there join the nun clapping and singing.

On the sidewalk, the kids draw houses, princesses, and hearts floating on strings like balloons. They remind me of my own eight-year-old daughter who selected the crayons, pads, and coloring books I brought to Nogales. But these migrant children face circumstances more difficult than anything my child or most of us have experienced. These children, from Mexico, Honduras, and Nicaragua, left everything to travel to a place they had never seen to escape life-threatening danger. And while theirs might seem like a familiar story in the myth of the American dream—the myth that anyone can make a better life here—quick comparisons mask the systemic discrimination and racism both particular to this moment and ingrained in US history.

Each body, each moment, each site of the present attaches to a past both individual and collective. Never a "neutral" record, the documentary poem might pull our bodies into other places not (just) in our imaginations, might open up possibilities for inquiry that shed light on a variety of archives beyond the control of the state. Not a court stenographer, the documentarian might also forgo the act of reportage to sit on the sidewalk and color in crayons, to forge a new relation.

33 *Zong! #1*

w w w w a wa

w a w a t

er wa s

our wa

te r gg g g go

o oo goo d

waa wa wa

w w waa

ter o oh

on o ne w one

w o n d d d

ey d a

dey a ah ay

s one day s

wa wa

Masuz Zuwena Ogunsheye Ziyad Ogwambi Keturah

34 M. NourbeSe Philip attempted to write a book documenting the massacre of some two-hundred enslaved Africans on board the slave ship Zong in 1781 using only a two-page legal document related to the event. She explains: "I initially tried many different techniques—cutting up the text; cutting holes in the text; whiting out and blacking out text—and trying to understand whether there was any difference created by the method of erasure. There were times when I absolutely panicked...."[35]

The document did not yield, until Philip vowed to trap herself in the body of the text "as if I had locked myself in the hold of the ship." After months of work and research, she began to cut into and apart the mere 500 words that constituted the entire legal document, rearranging the words and letters to fashion the poems and stories of the murdered slaves, channeling an experience in order to conjure the full catastrophe.

As the process unfolded, Philip sought permission to use these stories and traveled to Ghana to visit a shrine close to one of the slave ports. She met with an elder to discuss her book, she made an offering to the shrine "and to all the lost souls of Zong!" The cover of *Zong!* includes the words: *As told to the author by Setaey Adamu Boateng*. "I come—albeit slowly—to the understanding that *Zong!* is hauntology;" Philip writes "it is a work of haunting, a wake of sorts, where the spectres of the undead make themselves present."

The sociologist Avery Gordon considers haunting a framework through which to understand social dynamics. She writes: "Haunting occurs on the terrain situated between our ability to conclusively describe the logic of Capitalism or State Terror, for example, and the various experiences of this logic, experiences that are more often than not partial, coded, symptomatic, contradictory, ambiguous."[36]

Philip's ethical channeling offers another potential methodology for the poet or documentarian. Her ethics stem from her research and sympathies, her willingness to visit archive and shrine. Like Philip we must understand the histories that shape and frame our logics, perceptions, and feelings. We must work to understand our positions within the relations of our hauntings. (Leave the dead alone, my mother once told me when she heard I was playing with a Ouija board. Now she is dead and speaks to me in dreams.)

To access the stories excluded from the text or trapped within them as poets and documentarians, we must investigate, must listen for the voices silenced from the page. Instead of shrinking from the violence of the archive, we can match it as Philip does, becoming medium for what has been silenced. We must imagine, but we cannot appropriate nor ventriloquize. We train ourselves to tune into alternative archives.

To access the messages erased or excluded from the document or archive, sometimes we must record the knowledge we receive from ghosts, gossip, dream, sensation, gut-talk, myth. Not all information looks like information, nor does all communication. Scientists have discovered trees "talk" through roots, owls warn through wingflash. Maybe rocks, too, vibrate in frequencies beyond our ears. Communication buzzes all around us unrecognized.

The writer Selah Saterstrom suggests a divinatory practice can be a model for this kind of poetics:

> "Disarray" is a good word for the configuration that snaps a reading into place. It is less a situation of a linear narrative becoming coherent from inside a mess of cards on the table, and more an experience of (and/or with) an entity composed of disarray: its superfluous, midnight verdant logic lighting up the guts with the tangle, the mess, the shambles. "Disarray" doesn't imply an absence of arrangement or disposition in a reading. I often picture it in this way: when the reader's mouth opens to express the oracular bloom she is internally tracking, the reader sings out the mouth: a flock of birds (augury). And this is the reading.[37]

Like the card reader, we must find ways to recognize "the tangle, the mess, the shambles," the web of relation and possibility between our own lives and the systems that bind us to each other as well as our capability to reimagine them. As the poet Kenji C. Liu points out: "Divination is an imprecise process. Even the question's suitability is in question."[38] As writers we should know the histories beyond our own limited experiences, like the card reader knows her tarot in order to "best position one's multiple selves in the guts of the flux. ...[So she is] able, through a variety of modes and practices, to offer visibility to some poignant patterns." And our readings should always be consensual.

Perhaps the poem marks one space to bring light to such patterns.

And if the crossroads are the zone of the divinatory, what is the border?

"The laboratory of our future," writes Charles Bowden.

35 On the banks of an Austin creek, I watched the poet/artist Cecilia Vicuña thread a string around branches, in between the fingers of the audience/participants gathered and cast it over the water's surface to watch it unfurl in the current. Later Vicuña told me: "All lines and all threads have the same property as words: the double possibility of uniting and dividing.... All these borders, all these lines are really a coming to terms with that paradox that you are negotiating at every instance: the possibility of uniting or separating, taking or giving."[39]

Vicuña not only works with thread but makes small sculptures constructed from what she encounters in situ. She calls them *precarios* or *basuritas* (little precarious things or trash) small documentary monuments not unlike the ephemeral altars and shrines Kapil creates in her performances and classrooms.

Vicuña's thread and Saterstrom's tangle wind toward what Muriel Rukeyser called "the web in which people suffering, find themselves." According to Rukeyser, in order "to learn the people, to dissect the web, one deals with the processes themselves. To know the processes and the machines of process: plane and dynamo, gun and dam."[40] In "The Book of the Dead," Rukeyser uses history, myth, testimony, interview and intervention, to respond to the vibrating textual tangle of the moment, to remember the uninterrupted chain of presence around a singular event and under the systems of oppression ("the processes and the machines of process") that shape the moment for all of us albeit in different measures.

To see the web as well as to make it manifest. To speak the webs that exist and to speak new webs of connection into existence. To speak with the vulnerability of thread. The casting of a web or thread like the casting of a "spell" from the Old English *spel(l)* "narration," of Germanic origin.

Everything leans, the Buddhists say.

36 At the Arizona Sonora Border Projects for Inclusion work center in Nogales, Sonora, in July 2017, I stand with a group of students and watch a man fit a Honduran boy with a prosthetic calf and foot. The boy lost the lower part of his leg falling off The Beast, the network of Mexican freight trains that run from the Guatemalan to the US border. No hero's journey. No ritual. *To cross*: "to traverse" or "to oppose or stand in the way of something."

I have no idea, and I do not rush to imagine, how any of it could feel. Which is not a turning away, which is the opposite of turning away: to stand in my own relational presence before what might be known or not known to me, to tremble in the tangle of compassion, complicity, opacity, and relation. The work center provides wheelchairs and prosthetics designed for Mexico and Central America, employs men and women with disabilities, and receives money from the US Northern Command among other donors.

The boy smiles as a man wraps the plaster around the stump of his leg.

I bring the boy onto the page in solidarity with ARSOBO's work. And yet, as I retrace the boy's smile with my words, I want to scratch out the feel-good story of perseverance that might make bearable our complicity as US citizens in his injury, the kind of story that might be heard listening to the so-called liberal radio (as we drive home from our jobs in the military-prison-industrial-educational-kleptocracy we mistake for a nation), the kind of story that makes us feel just good enough to do nothing to alter our government's policies and our participation in the economics that create the conditions which forced the boy to heave his body up onto the train.

The screech of train brakes sounds like a scream, a scream like the sound of tons of steel and petroleum, commerce and indifference, grinding to a halt.

Economies will not be separated by a wall. Our appetites and negligence fuel a system as entangled as the orange trumpet vines growing up our desert fences.

I think again of the human cage through which the deported migrant walks making part of a public art installation, the poem at the port of entry that reads: "The border is what joins us, / Not what separates us."

I want poems to tell the story of the border without the comfort of resolution. I do not want to make disaster pornography but to make our responsibility in the atrocity of the border feel unbearable.

What are the aesthetics of no intelligibility, no relief?

"(I) worry about healing," writes poet Jenif(f)er Tamayo in her chapbook *to kill the future in the present*, which reverberates with her and her mother's own immigration detention. "every day i worry about the grounds that healing solidifies," she continues "who will be the last to heal? who will be forgotten in this healing process? i am not sure how healing is anything but a greater commitment to this very world before us. i want to resist the imperative to heal..."[41]

Perhaps the poem or the documentary can be a place to model not healing but discomfort with the wreckage of late capitalism and late empire, to model Agee's tremble, creating conditions for identification as well as difference and disambiguation, where contact and similitude are negotiated because it is only from the recognition of specific conditions that we can understand, work toward, or reject a reality, that we might rebuild this world.

Sometimes it helps to sit inside a building and imagine what it would be like to wreckingball its walls, in order to make sense of one's orientation.

As Tamayo writes: "in other words, i don't want to live forever/ i want new ways of living/ like, no, to this fucking air."

37 Venn diagrams make the world look orderly, when we might need to learn

to find our ever-shifting place in the tremble of our tangles.

38

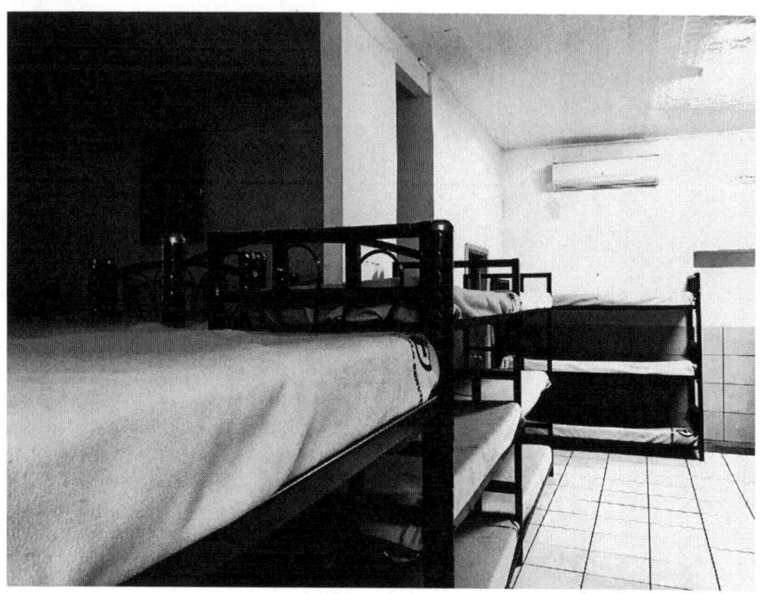

39 We stand at the front of the chapel, next to the small altar. Our guide at the Juan Bosco Migrant Shelter in Nogales, Sonora thought we (two men and three women from a university an hour to the north) were going to ask questions of the migrants seated in rows of folding chairs before us. But we stand before them silent. A door in the room's back wall remains open to the sidewalk; a fan vacillates near the altar. After a few awkward seconds, we ask the men and the women if they want to share anything with us. Most have either been deported or arrested on their journey, will be allowed to stay in the shelter until they can find work or another place to go. In the front row, two young girls flip through a blank notebook passing it back and forth between them.

And the men and women begin to call out from their folding chairs.

"The US officials take our documents and don't give them back," a woman says.

"They stick their hands in our mouth," she continues.

"They treat us like criminals," a man says.

And the men and women say "inhuman." They say "respect."

"Think of all the money they spend to pursue and prosecute us," one man says, "when all we want to do is work."

No one needs to prod them into speaking. They testify as we stand next to the altar, nodding and translating, holding our notebooks without remembering to write anything down.

And when they stop speaking, we thank them.

Before we leave, one of us pulls a pen out from her bag and hands it to the little girls, holding their own blank notebook in the first row of chapel.

But the story can't end here.

The pen is not a metaphor for giving voice. The pen is not a metaphor for giving tools. A tool is the flag hung over the water barrel or the coordinates of the barrel written into the code and transmitted to the migrant's phone or the poem that helps the migrant locate the north star.

Let us think, instead, about the blank notebook passed back and forth as promise, as the space to hear the vibrations of the relational web, to witness the wingflash, to resist the impulse to commodify a history of survival, to remember our place in relation and our potential to recognize

what haunts, what calls, what pecks at our awareness, what sings out or screams through the text of our present.

Let us think about the gift of the pen as a pledge to mark our silence before the stories that are not ours.

The pen is less important than what happens when we walk out of that room with the memory of those children.

To leave the page blank. To lay down. To see in the charged colors. To look directly into the camera. To be connected by more than flows of currencies. To turn our eyes towards the tangle: the webs of capitalism, antiblackness, white supremacy, narrative webs that constitute the veil of a military-prison-industrial-educational-kleptocracy we mistake for our democracy, the veil of silence and myth of voice, the commodity of story. To learn to recognize webs of need and responsibility, veil of the individual, the veil of racism, sexism, imperialism denying our humanity, our web of connections and differences, veils of deception and greed. To find the documents excluded from the archive, the stories in our cards and from our ancestors (what gets passed down or forgotten in the project of healing, who stares out the window and drinks themselves to rag), to remember that our stories do not take up equal space in the "marketplace" or the myth of the nation, that everyone has the right to their opacities, the beautiful eclipses

that both farmer and astrologer read.

Poems, documentaries, performances, (Soma)tics, rituals and divinatory readings can be a map or a code of coordinates. They might shine like guide-stars. And while they might not lead anyone to water, they might help them understand where they are and how they might change what surrounds them.

Our poems, documentaries, performances, (Soma)tics, rituals and divinatory readings might make a space like an empty notebook passed between sisters or friends

upon which they might leave their marks across a page or leave nothing but the space for someone else to write their story

a blank page, where anything is possible.

The bullet holes on the water station sign and the legal threats hurled at the "Desert Survival Series" remind us when our poems counter state sanctioned violence they will be challenged, not made part of the installation at the point of entry.

We must not make the suffering of others a commodity.

We must not seek the approval of the state or its co-conspirators.

We do not need more poems at the port of entry any more than we need the concertina wire that now sparkles like tinsel through Nogales.

We need people to bring the wall down.

40 In the final row of the US District Court, Arizona District, courtroom with my notebook and draft calendar, I am aware of how the state curates the image of seven men standing before the judge shackled at the wrists, waists, and ankles, how the state does not allow me to catch more than a glimpse of their faces, how the state renders them "undocumented" or "illegal" in its desire to create a link between brown bodies and criminality.

But this book can leave you with a counterimage:

A woman in a black strapless dress and black heels, paused halfway up a ladder perched along the US-Mexico border wall separating Playas de Tijuana from the San Diego Border Field State Park. With a paint gun, the Mexican artist Ana Teresa Fernández turns the metal bars of the fence to a pale powder blue until the fence itself seems to disappear:

a glimpse of a future.

FOR FURTHER STUDY (AN INVITATION TO SOMETHING OTHER THAN A MIRROR)

Declare a place of origin that cannot be found on any map.

Write the sound of a wall that is not raised.

Make a map without lines.

Write what you see when you lay your body down upon a geography that dreams

NOTES: GUIDESTARS, TANGLES, HAUNTOLOGIES

[25] *Transborder Immigrant Tool / La herramienta transfronteriza para inmigrantes*, 3.

[26] In addition to the *Transborder Immigrant Tool* itself, readers interested in the process of the app's and poems' creation should look to the October 15, 2011 interview with Ricardo Dominguez and other members of the Electronic Disturbance Theater in the online journal *Furtherfield*, as well as the essay "Trans of Color Poetics: Stitching Bodies, Concepts, and Algorithms" by micha cárdenas in *The Scholar & Feminist Online* journal.

[27] *Transborder Immigrant Tool / La herramienta transfronteriza para inmigrantes*, 52.

[28] Raquel Gutierrez, "I Pledge Allegiance To *THIS* Flag: Arivaca Riding with Humane Borders," *Field Studies Writing Blog*, (July 12, 2017): web.

[29] From Bhanu Kapil's *Ban en banlieue*, 16: "2. Street: Lie down on sidewalk next to the ivy in the exact spot that the novel is set, somewhere between Balmoral Avenue and Landsbury Drive. Observe the sky: Install circular mirrors in the vines. Nervous system notes. Descriptions of the weather and neighborhood. Similarly, at other sites in West London, crumple aluminum foil, make a daffodil ikebana as a late April shine. Hayes, Middlesex, England, 2012"

[30] *Ibid*, 59.

[31] During a March 13, 2014 reading at the University of Arizona Poetry Center, Conrad explained: "I come from a working-class community in rural Pennsylvania. And when I was growing up, I wanted nothing to do with the factory." Conrad came from a family of factory workers whom they described as "fairly miserable people." Returning from a visit with family, they explained: "I realized that I had turned my poetry into an assembly line, ...I stopped writing because I didn't want to be part of a factory." They wrote a list of the things that were wrong with the factory top among them was "The inability to be present." Conrad explains: "My father never was in the present. He was never there when he was there. Why would he be. He hated his job."

[32] CA Conrad, "(Soma)tic Poetry Rituals: The Basics in 3 Parts," *(Soma)tic Poetry Rituals Blog*, (Aug 18, 2018): web.

[33] Édouard Glissant, *The Poetics of Relation*, (Ann Arbor, MI: Univ of Michigan Press, 1997), 191.

[34] Mark Nowak, "Panthers, Patriots, and Poetry in Revolution," *Organize Your Own*, (December 12, 2016): web.

[35] Andrew David King, "The Weight of What's Left Out: Six Contemporary Erasurists on Their Craft," *The Kenyon Review Blog*, (November 6, 2012): web.

[36] Avery Gordon, *Ghostly Matters*, (Minneapolis: University of Minnesota Press, 2008), 24.

[37] Selah Saterstrom, *Ideal Suggestions: Essays in Divinatory Poetics* (Essay Press, 2017), xxi.

[38] Kenji C. Liu, *Craters a field guide* (Goodmorning Menagerie, 2017), 26

[39] Susan Briante, "Seeing and Gathering," *The Texas Observer* (May 21, 2004): web.

[40] Muriel Rukeyser, *Willard Gibbs*, (Garden City, New York: Doubleday and Co., 1942), 12.

[41] Jennif(f)er Tamayo, *to kill the future in the present*, (Chicago: Green Lantern Press, 2018), 17.

EPILOGUE:

ROLLING

[redacted]

STOPPED CLOCKS, [redacted] **VIDEOS** [redacted]

night stand
2 tissue boxes hospital issue
St. Josephs Statue
Coupon Cafe Gallo -
bookmark - St. Therese
"I well spread my heaven, doing good on earth" "Rosemarie"
- two padre pio mass card
- prayers + devotions for health + healing - Our Lady of Lourds
- prayer to St Monica, to St Michaele to St. Jude to our lady of sorrows

When my mother died, I took a photograph of all the objects she left on the mirror tray on her dresser. I made a list of all the books, papers, and magazines found on her reading table:

Penny's Finest Favorite Word Series Word Seeks for Everyone
Anticancer A New Way of Life
Article ripped from a magazine "Shiny bouncy hair"
Article rippled from a magazine "Fine/Thick Haircare Products"
TV Guide for the week of Sunday, Sept 28, 2014
3 months *Redbook* magazines
Photocopied essay "What Motherhood Really Means to Me" author unknown
Article: "Heat or Ice" *AARP*
"Derek Jeter Before his Final Home Game Looks Back on his Hudson County Roots" printed from *NJ.com*
Penny Press Goodtime Easy Crosswords
Card hand-drawn from her granddaughter Gianna with pressed leaf and stick inside

I recorded all the items on her nightstand, next to the bed where she had not slept in weeks, where I would sleep uneasily while she lay in hospice: every piece of clothing or costume jewelry that she would never wear again vibrating in the room around me.

Do they vibrate still without either of us near?

On the day my mother died, I only opened my computer twice: once at 1:36 pm and again at 7:13 pm. According to my Google search history, I looked at my email account, looked at my university home page, the weather. On the day after her death, I looked at celebrity hairstyles in the late afternoon after shopping for wine for the repast. I looked at celebrity Halloween costumes, *Elle*'s celebrity hair transformations, the NEA website. I booked flights for my husband and daughter to attend her funeral.

In the days after her death, I take notes on the days before her death when I visited her in hospice:

Monday: arrival
Tuesday: struggle for words, friends come, gasping choking
Wednesday: no words, swabs in the mouth
Thursday: dies in the morning

In a black binder clip in the top desk drawer of my home office, I keep the essay "What Motherhood Really Means to Me," a list of her symptoms, a list of her medication in my father's handwriting (his "*a*" will never be seen again), the mass card from her funeral, a boarding pass from my Tucson to Newark flight.

I do not know what I am saving them for. I do not know what story I hope to tell about capitalism or family, mothering or money, about cancer (from the Latin word for *crab*, because cancer cells scuttle throughout the body, forget their function, and place). I wear my mother's ring, not because I like it, but because when I look down, I see her fingers on my hand.

The mirror tray on her dresser was a wedding gift from her grandmother that came with a matching clock. The clock now sits on a shelf in my living room even though it has stopped.

* 

Experts in authoritarianism advise to keep a list of things subtly changing around you, so you'll remember. Here's my list for week 2:
1. The First Family-elect will not be living in the White House.
2. Melania's bio changed overnight to reflect she did not go to college.
3. Donald Jr. met with Russia representatives in Paris to discuss Syria during the election.
4. Aleppo has devolved into the worst humanitarian crisis in our lifetimes,and Putin is emboldened to tell the US to stay out.
5. Putin has moved missiles in Kaliningrad "in response to NATO aggression" - within striking distance of Germany.
6. Russian propaganda was the source of much of the "fake news" during the campaign.
7. Trump has selectively been meeting with the media and grooming them by yelling at them. They all showed up for this.
8. Next day he met with the NYT at their offices, and their coverage totally normalized his porous positions and outrageous actions so far.
9. Trump has been furthering his business affairs and using his presidency to get licenses and other favors.
10. His daughter Ivanka and son-in-law Jared have joined him in meetings and calls with heads of state, and other senior officials from other countries.
11. Trump openly stated that he doesn't care about conflicts of interest, and he does not feel compelled in any way to separate his business dealings from his role as president.
12. Trump admitted to breaking the law! He signed off on Trump Foundation's tax statement and now has admitted the Foundation was in violation of tax laws.
13. In Wisconsin, 5k of Trump's 27k vote lead have been proven to be fake votes.
14. In true dictatorial form, Trump demands Mitt Romney publicly apologize if he wants the position of Secretary of State.
15. Trump is selling Trump merchandise in Trump Tower and online, including Christmas tree ornaments.
16. CNN airs a segment with subline, "Are Jews People."
17. Hate crimes continue nationwide against Muslims, Jews, women, Black and Hispanic Americans. On a Delta flight, one Trump supporter screamed at Hillary bitches, and didn't get kicked off.
18. Steve Bannon received $376k from a small Foundation in Tallahassee to pay a salary for his work at Breidbart.
I'm sure there are more. This list is overwhelming already.

IIII

In the weeks after Donald Trump was declared President of the United States after failing to win the popular vote with the assistance of Russian actors who "intervened in the election through a variety of means,"[42] articles on how to survive authoritarianism circulated on US media platforms.[43] Journalist and author Sarah Kendzior published one in *de Correspondent* in which she urged Americans to "write about who you are, what you have experienced, and what you have endured." Kendzior warned:

> Write down what you value; what standards you hold for yourself and for others.
>
> Write a list of things you would never do...
>
> Write a list of things you would never believe...
>
> It is increasingly clear, as Donald Trump appoints his cabinet of white supremacists and warmongers, as hate crimes rise, as the institutions that are supposed to protect us cower, as international norms are shattered, that his ascendency to power is not normal.[44]

Activist and writer Amy Siskind took up the challenge of documenting exactly what was "not normal" on November 20, 2016 and began to compile a weekly list initially published on Facebook of all of the legal and political conventions Trump violated.[45] They read as notes without sources, written quickly with emotion ("Trump admitted to breaking the law!"). The lists went viral, and Siskind compiled them into a book published in March 2018. They continue today as part of the website *The Weekly List* (theweeklylist.org), which "tracks specific news stories representing eroding norms under the current regime." The website claims: "Taken together, they reveal a nation pushed toward authoritarianism."

IIII

As the handheld video begins, the viewer sees through a doorway two armed and uniformed Border Patrol agents standing in front of a projection of the Border Patrol shield at the head of a classroom on the University of Arizona campus. "Murderers," the woman filming with her phone begins her narration, "I don't know who allowed the murder patrols... murderers on campus where I pay to be here."[46]

The woman filming pans in and out quickly on the agents, appears to open the door wider. "Murderers on campus," she repeats, "where I pay to be here. This is supposed to be a safe place on campus."

Her voice gets louder as she continues filming and speaking. "How about you talk about slashing water [bottles], taking the shoes off migrants and letting them walk through the desert?"

A student from inside the classroom, a member of the Criminal Justice Association, the club that invited the Border Patrol to give a presentation, approaches the student filming. The student filming says to her: "You as a club should be more conscious that students need to feel safe on this campus and maybe find a meeting place outside..."

The woman from inside the classroom says: "If you don't feel safe, I will call the UAPD."

"You think the UAPD is going to make me feel safe?" the student filming responds. "White woman calling the police."

The two agents shake hands with the students from the club standing at the door and start to walk out of the classroom. At this point, other voices join the student who began filming in the chant: "Murder Patrol. Murder Patrol." They continue chanting and following the officers. She films the agents, whose guns can clearly be seen, as they walk down hallways and out to the parking garage.

The video cuts to the officers entering their car. Her voice becoming hoarse, the student filming screams: "A la verga con la migra!"

IIII

In a dream, all of my father's clothes lay on a bed; his ties hang from a plastic hanger; his white sneakers, his loafers, his slippers lined up against a wall. His closets are empty and open. In truth, there's a part of me that wishes I had kept every one of his shirts, his socks, and his shoehorn, everything he touched. I remember how awful it felt stuffing all of my mother's clothes into black garbage bags to donate to charity. But every year it seems I am still giving away one more piece of her clothing I thought I would wear.

Gone, slurred over to another form.

When my father died, I took photographs of every room in his house.

My ability to touch anything that once belonged to my parents (the small plastic portfolio with her grandchildren's school photos; his calendar, his address books): a privilege.

xylophagia: a desire to eat pencils or paper
photophagia: a desire to eat photographs

In the dream, my mother asks me what I am doing with all of my father's clothes. I tell her with a kind of exhaustion: I miss him.

IIII

Timothy Snyder updated his status.
November 15, 2016 ·

Americans are no wiser than the Europeans who saw democracy yield to fascism, Nazism, or communism. Our one advantage is that we might learn from their experience. Now is a good time to do so. Here are twenty lessons from the twentieth century, adapted to the circumstances of today.

1. Do not obey in advance. Much of the power of authoritarianism is freely given. In times like these, individuals think ahead about what a more repressive government will want, and then start to do it without being asked. You've already done this, haven't you? Stop. Anticipatory obedience teaches authorities what is possible and accelerates unfreedom.

2. Defend an institution. Follow the courts or the media, or a court or a newspaper. Do not speak of "our institutions" unless you are making them yours by acting on their behalf. Institutions don't protect themselves. They go down like dominoes unless each is defended from the beginning.

3. Recall professional ethics. When the leaders of state set a negative example, professional commitments to just practice become much more important. It is hard to break a rule-of-law state without lawyers, and it is hard to have show trials without judges.

4. When listening to politicians, distinguish certain words. Look out for the expansive use of "terrorism" and "extremism." Be alive to the fatal notions of "exception" and "emergency." Be angry about the treacherous use of patriotic vocabulary.

5. Be calm when the unthinkable arrives. When the terrorist attack comes, remember that all authoritarians at all times either await or plan such events in order to consolidate power. Think of the Reichstag fire. The sudden disaster that requires the end of the balance of power, the end of opposition parties, and so on, is the oldest trick in the Hitlerian book. Don't fall for it.

6. Be kind to our language. Avoid pronouncing the phrases everyone else does. Think up your own way of speaking, even if only to convey that thing you think everyone is saying. (Don't use the internet before bed. Charge your gadgets away from your bedroom, and read.) What to read? Perhaps "The Power of the Powerless" by Václav Havel, 1984 by George Orwell, The Captive Mind by Czesław Milosz, The Rebel by Albert Camus, The Origins of Totalitarianism by Hannah Arendt, or Nothing is True and Everything is Possible by Peter Pomerantsev.
7. Stand out. Someone has to. It is easy, in words and deeds, to follow along. It can feel strange to do or say something different. But without that unease, there is no freedom. And the moment you set an example, the spell of the status quo is broken, and others will follow.
8. Believe in truth. To abandon facts is to abandon freedom. If nothing is true, then no one can criticize power, because there is no basis upon which to do so. If nothing is true, then all is spectacle. The biggest wallet pays for the most blinding lights.
9. Investigate. Figure things out for yourself. Spend more time with long articles. Subsidize investigative journalism by subscribing to print media. Realize that some of what is on your screen is there to harm you. Learn about sites that investigate foreign propaganda pushes.
10. Practice corporeal politics. Power wants your body softening in your chair and your emotions dissipating on the screen. Get outside. Put your body in unfamiliar places with unfamiliar people. Make new friends and march with them.
11. Make eye contact and small talk. This is not just polite. It is a way to stay in touch with your surroundings, break down unnecessary social barriers, and come to understand whom you should and should not trust. If we enter a culture of denunciation, you will want to know the psychological landscape of your daily life.
12. Take responsibility for the face of the world. Notice the swastikas and the other signs of hate. Do not look away and do not get used to them. Remove them yourself and set an example for others to do so.

IIII

Theorists understand trauma (See: *An Archive of Feelings: Trauma, Sexuality, and Lesbian Public Cultures* and *Depression: A Public Feeling.*) as overwhelming or unbearable experience that cannot be integrated into the subject's ongoing narrative of their lives. While the diagnostic definition of trauma traces its origins to "actual or threatened death, serious injury, or sexual violence," scholars such as Ann Cvetkovich have looked at how microagressions as well as quotidian and insidious psychic violence (produced by capitalism, misogyny, racism, homophobia, etc.) can impact individuals in ways best understood through the lens of trauma.

Is it possible to consider Trump's ascension to power as a traumatic event?

Yes.

For one quarter of the university students surveyed in a recent study, the 2016 election caused stress levels comparable to those of witnesses to a mass shooting.[47]

Perhaps, more importantly, we might consider the relationship between the need to document our stories in times of heightened trauma including the Trump presidency.

I don't mean to suggest documentary list making is a kind of "talking cure" in which the narrativization of traumatic events will lead to their integration. Rather, we counteract the false appearance of normalcy. When we document, we contest the echo chamber of news outlets that repeat the lies of the state or promote points of view that benefit a (mostly) white elite and their financial interests.[48] We begin a process that allows us to reframe and recontextualize every exception and every unexceptional atrocity.

In 1936, Wallace Stevens wrote that "in the presence of extraordinary actuality, consciousness takes the place of the imagination." Noting a turn toward the documentary in a variety of arts including poetry, Stevens explained the Depression had focused everyone's attention "in the direction of reality, that is to say in the direction of fact."[49]

A cataloguing impulse forms part of documentary works as different as Bernadette Mayer's *Midwinter Day* (in its meticulous documentation of one day in the poet's life, which Alice Notley called "an epic poem about an ordinary day") and Claudia Rankine's *Citizen* (in its offering of case after case of antiblack violence and microaggression, which has become one of the most widely read books of poetry in recent years).

The documentary list making promoted by Kendzior and enacted by Siskind provides a way to bring abnormalities and abominations to the surface of our consciousness in order that we might organize to resist them collectively. In his book *On Tyranny: Twenty Lesson from the Twentieth Century,* historian Timothy Snyder reminds us: "Think up your own way of speaking. When we repeat the same words and phrases that appear in the daily media, we accept the absence of a larger framework." With his call to "[t] hink up your own way of speaking," Snyder brings to mind Philip's wrecking re-creation of the language of law to bring forth the silenced voices of the Zong. I imagine Snyder's framework extending like Rukeyser's web of connections in which we might understand our place and power in relation to suffering.

IIII

Case Summary Report

Agency: UAPD **Case Number:** 1903250006 **Date:** 4/12/2019 08:33:32
Last Modified: 4/5/2019 15:21:40

Notes/Narratives

I did activate my BWC for this incident.

On 03-19-19 at 1658 hours I responded to the Modern Languages building, room 304 reference a female causing a disturbance. Upon arrival I observed a female dressed in a black shirt and black jeans yelling from the hallway (leaning forward to get her head inside the classroom). The female continuously yelled "murder patrol". Inside the classroom I saw there were about 10 college aged people seated and at the front of the class there were two Border Patrol agents. I then spoke t advised the room was being used for a club sponsored Criminal Justice even advised the female had been yelling for approximately 20 minutes. The agents were trying to continue with their presentation; however, the female was very loud and it caused the presentation to be disrupted. There was a male who said his name is and he was from the Chavez building, but I am not sure what his role was or why he was there.

The female was soon joined by a second female who started yelling "murder patrol". I asked them both to step back and tried to reason with them. I told them there was a better way to get their point across. I told them they were disrupting the event and asked them to stop. Both females ignored me and continued to yell at the agents. Along with shouting murder patrol they also yelled "how many children were taken from their family an hour ago". I requested my supervisor to respond, see Cpl Pickrom`s supplements. I had dispatch contact the on duty Dean of Students to advise them of the situation.

Via the telephone I spoke with Dea for some guidance advised me to again ask them to stop and let them know there is a more educated way to protest. I attempted to again reason with them and once again they ignored my request. By this time a third female joined the other two and all were repeatedly yelled "murder patrol". Once Cpl Pickrom arrived I handed my cell phone to him so he could speak with the Dean. After speaking with the Dean Cpl Pickrom said he wanted both exit/entry doors closed. We closed both doors, this did not stop the three females from shouting, directed at the agents. I heard one of the females yell "get the fuck off my campus". I am not sure which one yelled this.

At around this time the Professor from across the hall, room came out and advised me and Cpl Pickrom the shouting had disrupted his class to the point where he could not continue to teach. In lieu of possibly escalating the incident I asked the Professor if he could move his class to another area. The Professor agreed and said he would take his students outside and teach from the courtyard. The Professor said his name was and it was class he was trying to teach. The agents presentation was supposed to go until 1800 hours, however, Cpl Pickrom asked them if they would end it early. The agents agreed and at 1748 hours the agents gather their things and left going towards the 2nd St garage Cpl Pickrom followed them to the garage and I stayed behind to ensure everyone left peacefully.

I did not get the name`s of any of the protesters. NFI.

IIII

In publishing online the video of border patrol agents, complete with her and others' chants of "Murder Patrol, Murder Patrol," the student who filmed becomes both documentarian and activist, taking up Snyder's charge "to find her own way of speaking." Her narration reminds us of the contested (if not criminal) border and immigration policies which force migrants to cross the desert in remote and dangerous terrain as well as the Border Patrol's legacy of thwarting any attempts to provide humanitarian aid.

Her video is a poem asking of its viewers the same questions over and over: Will you continue to support our violent policies on the border? ("like, no, to this fucking air.")

And for such documentation and activism, this student and two other University of Arizona students face misdemeanor charges for "interference with the peaceful conduct of an educational institution," carrying up to six months in jail. The student who filmed the incident is charged additionally with "threats and intimidation," another misdemeanor.[50]

Like Kapil and Conrad, she places her body into sites of confrontation and investigation. Like Rukeyser, **she defaces the document, even the document she makes, unsettling the narratives of the state.**

IIII

My father kept manila folders labeled with the names of utility companies or credit cards where he filed the bills he paid with the date and number of the checks he wrote logged on each. My father retired in 2001, never worked a job in which he used a laptop or desktop computer. He once told me a key to efficiency in business was to never touch the same paper twice.

In the weeks after my father's death, I am sick with grief and with the sight of my desk covered in papers and receipts. Like him, I want to document what debt I carry, what I have paid. But my debt extends in ways my father never understood. As Cristina Rivera Garza explains:

> When we write, we write with others. Inescapably. If we write, we write about others, even when we write about ourselves in small diaries that remain hidden in locked drawers. Constantly borrowing from the language we share with entire and varied communities at once, when we write we acquire a debt—a real, material debt—with the practitioners of such languages. It's an immense debt. It is, as Fred Moten and Stefano Harney argued in *The Undercommons,* a debt that is or will become unpayable. We cannot hide it or deny it. The only thing left to do is increase it.[51]

Sometimes I return to the papers, receipts, texts, notebooks, word docs and videos of my archive in order to understand their limits and their sources as I try to trace what I owe to community of writers around me.

My parents were often suspicious of that which was not like them: my non-Italian American friends, my queer, my loves, my career, my critique, my resistance, my view of a world they could not see. Perhaps the best thing they taught me was to distrust any one singular view of the world.

Recently, we learned my paternal great-grandfather was an orphan, found in a baby-hatch in Caposele, Italy. What do you call someone who cannot speak and comes without a name? Maria Spatola, the midwife who discovered him, decided upon Alfonso Ebriante.

In some version of this book all the text would be erasable, every line open to your revision.

IIII

When the university releases the names of the student protestors, they receive death threats. Threats against the Department of Mexican American Studies lead to the department's evacuation. During that same week in the Spring 2019, the University of Arizona chapter of the College Republicans invites Art Del Cueto, Vice-President and Spokesperson from the Border Patrol Council, to speak on campus. With the help of the right-wing group Judicial Watch, Del Cueto lead a movement on conservative media outlets calling for the UA administration to press charges against the students who protested the Border Patrol.

Still many faculty and students support the actions of the student who filmed and protested the Border Patrol's presence as well as the others who joined her. UA professor and essayist Fenton Johnson writes University of Arizona President Robert C. Robbins to explain how the presence of uniformed and armed agents could not only be seen as a provocation, but as a disturbance in and of itself.

Johnson explains:

> ...They, and/or the faculty who invited them, should have been sensitive to the predictable and distressing impact of their appearing as a uniformed phalanx. Having been given no context for their visit, I immediately and reasonably assumed they were on campus to detain students whom they believed to be undocumented. I retreated from the hallway to my classroom because, in effect, I decided that was the best way to protect students who might be their target.
>
> I don't know what I would have done had the officers knocked at my classroom door, but it was that prospect, not the demonstration, that distracted me from teaching my course.[52]

Johnson concludes his letter expressing admiration for the students. "...[W]e should be grateful to them for drawing attention to a serious lacuna in University policies and procedures."

How do we document what might seem "unimaginable" to some?

How do we use the documents we have to imagine something else?

IIII

I used to flinch at my parents' narrations. "Remember when you had your fit?" my mother says referencing the seizures I had as a child, days redacted from a calendar. Now my parents can no longer fill in the blanks of my stories. I know no one alive who was present at my birth. But I am no longer vulnerable to their narratives about me.

When I write I miss my parents, it is not without remembering all the storm and hurt of our relationship. When I mourn my parents, I mourn the possibility that they might have loved me as I needed to be loved.

When I write miss my country, I mourn the possibility of what this country could provide for everyone.

And then I wonder: why do we need countries?

IIII
U.S. Department of Justice
~~Attorney Work Product~~ // ~~May Contain Material Protected Under Fed. R. Crim. P. 6(e)~~

b. Contacts with the Campaign about WikiLeaks

Harm to Ongoing Matter [193] Harm to Ongoing Matter On June 12, 2016, Assange claimed in a televised interview to "have emails relating to Hillary Clinton which are pending publication,"[194] but provided no additional context.

In debriefings with the Office, former deputy campaign chairman Rick Gates said that, Harm to Ongoing Matter [195] Harm to Ongoing Matter Gates recalled candidate Trump being generally frustrated that the Clinton emails had not been found.[196]

Paul Manafort, who would later become campaign chairman, Harm to Ongoing Matter .[197] Harm to Ongoing Matter [198]

---

[193] Harm to Ongoing Matter

[194] *See* Mahita Gajanan, *Julian Assange Timed DNC Email Release for Democratic Convention*, Time (July 27, 2016) (quoting the June 12, 2016 television interview).

[195] In February 2018, Gates pleaded guilty, pursuant to a plea agreement, to a superseding criminal information charging him with conspiring to defraud and commit multiple offenses (*i.e.*, tax fraud, failure to report foreign bank accounts, and acting as an unregistered agent of a foreign principal) against the United States, as well as making false statements to our Office. Superseding Criminal Information, *United States v. Richard W. Gates III*, 1:17-cr-201 (D.D.C. Feb. 23, 2018), Doc. 195 ("*Gates* Superseding Criminal Information"); Plea Agreement, *United States v. Richard W. Gates III*, 1:17-cr-201 (D.D.C. Feb. 23, 2018), Doc. 205 ("*Gates* Plea Agreement"). Gates has provided information and in-court testimony that the Office has deemed to be reliable.

[196] Gates 10/25/18 302, at 1-2.

[197] As explained further in Volume I, Section IV.A.8, *infra*, Manafort entered into a plea agreement with our Office. We determined that he breached the agreement by being untruthful in proffer sessions and before the grand jury. We have generally recounted his version of events in this report only when his statements are sufficiently corroborated to be trustworthy; to identify issues on which Manafort's untruthful responses may themselves be of evidentiary value; or to provide Manafort's explanations for certain events, even when we were unable to determine whether that explanation was credible. His account appears here principally because it aligns with those of other witnesses.

[198] Grand Jury

52

IIII

Black bars on the police report, black paragraphs on the Special Investigator's report, black bars like those graffitied across the hills of Nogales, all absence, all that will forever remain unsaid between my parents and me.

IIII

While many of Trump's policies and actions mark a radical departure from norms as well as the rule of law, some represent a continuation of longstanding approaches. For example, Operation Streamline began under President George W. Bush and continued during the Obama administration.

The policy of separating children from their parents at the border has decades of precedent in different forms including the mass-deportations of Mexican immigrants that took place during the Great Depression.[53] Slavery, Indian Boarding Schools, and early twentieth-century immigration policies that turned away the sick, all resulted in children being ripped away from their parents. Despite our myths or aspirations, the United States has implemented policies that destroy families—especially families of color—since our founding.

IIII

Hundreds of UA faculty, staff, and students as well as community members march silently across the UA campus, dressed in white, holding signs that say: "The Border Patrol is the Disruption" and "Drop the Charges: No ICE No Border Patrol on Campus."

I carry my sign. I remain silent as the woman from NPR shoves a microphone in my face. I walk before the President's desk.

I add my name to the petition created by the Arizona ACLU. I call the Pima County Attorney's Office. I contact colleagues at other universities and hold conference calls with PEN America.

Letters arrive from faculty across the UA campus and from other institutions. *Salon, Teen Vogue, The Guardian* and *Democracy Now* run stories about the students, now known as The Arizona 3.

Within a few weeks, the County Attorney drops the charges and refers the matter to the Dean of Students who continues to investigate. The students and their supporters express relief but now push for the removal of Border Patrol or ICE officials from campus and a formal apology from the president.

Still, four Arizona State legislators release a statement criticizing the Pima County Attorney's decision and standing with the University police chief in charging "those who disrupt the process of learning." Among their threats, they claim: "If it becomes necessary to terminate the employment of professors, tenured or not, for interfering with university operations, we will stand with President Robbins and the decisions he makes."[54] As of this writing, the administration has not discussed any such terminations.

IIII

In the book I read with my daughter, a child wants to go back in time to right his father's mistakes. In another book, a child erases her parents' memory of her to protect them.

What tricks or twists, what bends of time do we wish to rend around us as we confront the unsolvable equations of *what might have been*?

In an archive, there should be an order, document follows document, but often we yearn to thwart chronology.

Why must our documents be coherent if order is what we want to disrupt?

IIII

When I told my daughter that her grandfather had died, she sobbed and held her head in her hands. "My little brain can't take it," she said. **"It's too much. It's too much."**

Our brains rewire themselves to accommodate an absence in the aftermath of death no matter what lists or mementos we have kept. I feel it in the struggle to not reach for the phone to call my mother every day after work, in the stories about my daughter I have no parent to share with. I feel it in the respite from my mother's anxiety, my father's critique, his bitter racism at the end of his life. I think of Bernadette Mayer who writes about her "failure to forget mother and father enough/...to remember their bigotry accurately."[55] The death of a parent like a regime change takes time to be incorporated into the narrative of our lives. With the death of my parents I am learning to mourn and grieve and question my own sentimentality. Perhaps without sentimentality for habits or institutions, we (as poets, as documentarians, as inhabitants or citizens) can learn to confront the regime change of 2016 as well as the continuation of foundational oppressions.

If trauma is that which we must integrate, we must also learn to make space for realities (traumatic and otherwise) that challenge our own racialized, class- or gender-based mythologies of normalcy. As poets and documentarians, we must learn to recognize the ways in which we unwittingly or wittingly contribute to the trauma of others, how we benefit from their oppression. We must reconfigure our notions of the document and the art we produce from it in order to reconfigure our world.

We must reckon with new worlds in our suffering, in the nightmare's expansion. But there is also space for imagining. All of my life I imagined the family I needed. Inside me: documents of possibility.

The week I begin to draft this chapter, Dr. Scott Warren, an activist with the group No More Deaths, faces felony charges and twenty years in prison for providing "food, water, and clean clothes" to migrants crossing the border between Arizona and Mexico.[56] In the same week, 200 students at Tucson's Desert View High School walk out in support of an undocumented classmate, who was picked up in a routine traffic stop and taken into Border Patrol custody.[57] The *Wall Street Journal* reports: "Arrests of families crossing the US-Mexico border illegally in the past five months hit a record, prompting the chief of Customs and Border Protection to say the system is at 'the breaking point.'"[58] And another 75 migrants are scheduled to stand before a judge in an Arizona courtroom in another day of Operation Streamline adding the words of "yes," "no" and "guilty" to the court record while nearly every other fact about them remains beyond the margins and outside the care of the system.

How can we digest it?

What are you tracking: ice melt, school shootings, the murders of trans-women or indigenous women, government corruption compounded each day?

"Widen the gaze," Rukeyser writes.

We need a kind of negative capability to deal with the present moment:

to see the present as another coordinate in a long history of racist, misogynist and capitalist oppression, without allowing the continued separation of families at our borders, the assault on women's rights (reproductive and otherwise), assaults on the rights of the LGBTQ+ community and their rights, the criminalization of nonwhite bodies, the criminalization of poverty, the continued destruction of our environment—to become any more normalized than they already are.

In the week I begin drafting this chapter, students at Johns Hopkins launch a sit-in occupation of their administration building, protesting their university's contracts with Immigrations and Customs Enforcement.[59] Students at San Jose City College organize until their administration rescinds an invitation to Border Patrol to appear at a campus job fair.[60] At Swarthmore College, students occupy a fraternity after a campus newspaper publishes leaked "meeting minutes" detailing sexual violence and racial prejudice by fraternity members. Within days, the only two fraternities on campus disband. As I complete this chapter, I think back over the past few months when protest movements in Puerto Rico force the resignation of a corrupt governor. More recently, mass mobilizations in Hong Kong lead the government to withdraw legislation that would allow extradition to China and have sparked a continuing pro-democracy movement.

We need to document. But without activism, the document (or the list) can become a source of nostalgia as useless as the stopped clock sitting on my living room shelf.

This country like a clock stopped.

With what methods will we push it forward?

The poem, the archive, the activism, in urgency and inquiry, in what Philip describes as the willingness to "to sail in the dark with no compass," in what the poet and activist Marianna Ariel called the "unknown and utterly necessary other thing our imaginations need to reach towards."[61]

The future unfurls like the sky above the cities of Nogales, Arizona, and Nogales, Sonora, a sky redacted by the bars of a wall.

What will we write or imagine between those bars? What will we make from them?

I used to believe the document tethered the poem to the earth, to soil that one could taste, that could be nutrient to more than one. Now I believe the document might be a lightning rod sometimes conducting the raw power of the state, sometimes the site of illumination or transformation.

I do not know what comes next or how we might confront it.

But I am sure that a desert does not need to be a weapon or a graveyard.

And a wall will not be the end.

NOTES: EPILOGUE: STOPPED CLOCKS, ROLLING VIDEOS

[42] Madeleine Carlisle and Olivia Paschal, "Read Robert Mueller's Written Summaries of His Russia Report" *Atlantic Online*, (April 18, 2019): web.

[43] These include "Autocracy: Rules for Survival" by Masha Gessen in the *New York Review of Books* and "Trump is following the authoritarian playbook" by Ruth Ben-Ghiat on *CNN.com*.

[44] Sarah Kendzior, "We're Heading into Dark Times. This is How to Be Your Own Light in the Age of Trump," *de Correspondent*, (November 18, 2016.): web.

[45] While the example of Siskind demonstrates that social media websites such as Facebook can provide valuable methods for sharing information to counter authoritarianism or support regime change, the algorithms in such social media servers can tailor "news content" to reinforce the beliefs of the user without safeguards as to whether the content has any basis in fact.

[46] The woman who took video of the Border Patrol officers on campus was an undergraduate at the University of Arizona at the time. Because of the harassment she received after the incident, including death-threats, I have chosen not to reprint her name here. All quotes have been transcribed from the video which I accessed online in May 2019.

[47] Jen Christensen, "College students experienced trauma symptoms after Trump's election, study says," *CNN.com*, (October 22, 2018): web.

[48] In *Carceral Capitalism*, Jackie Wang notes the narratives promoted by the corporate media often delineate the limits of our political imagination. She writes:

> The media construction of urban ghettos and prisons as "alternate universes" marks them as zones of unintelligibility, faraway places removed from the everyday white experience. Native American reservations are another example of' "void" zones that white people can only access through the fantasy of media representation. What happens in these zones of abjection and vulnerability does not typically register in the white imaginary.

The border is another zone of unintelligibility for the non-white body. ICE and Border Patrol policing have extended the border throughout the whole country.

[49] As quoted in William Stott's *Documentary Expression in Thirties America*, 119.

[50] On March 21, two days after a UA student filmed border patrol agents screaming out a larger framework for their presence from a university doorframe, Art Del Cueto, Vice-President and Spokesperson for the Border Patrol Council, began talking about the incident on right-wing

radio and podcasts: "[She] was stalking. She was harassing Border Patrol Agents... they did not provoke her in any way." On one of these shows, Del Cueto threatens the student with physical violence ("I would have punched her") as well as intimidation ("I want to see if anyone in her family has done anything illegal"). Del Cueto threatened the University as well: "I am hoping that UA responds and shows their support for law enforcement and these agents... In the past, the Department of Homeland security has donated millions of dollars in research." On March 25, the conservative activist group, Judicial Watch, sent a letter to President Robbins, co-signed by Del Cueto, declaring the students' behavior was "in conflict with and in violation UA's code of conduct as well as laws."

Four days later, UA President Robbins announced charges would be filed a gainst t he students.

51 Cristina Rivera Garza, "The Unusual: A Manifesto," *Pen Transmissions*, (May 17, 2018): web.

52 Fenton Johnson, "Fenton Johnson's Letter to University of Arizona's President Robbins Regarding #TheArizona3," *Medium*, (April 17, 2019).

53 See Paul Fass's "If You're Shocked by Reports on Children at the Border, You Haven't Paid Attention to American History," *Time*, (July 11, 2019) and Natalie Escobar's "Child Separation Isn't New," *The Atlantic*, (Aug 14, 2019).

54 Representatives Leo Biasiucci, Mark Finchem and Bret Roberts and Senator Vince Leach, "Legistlators Criticize Pima County Attorney's Decision to Dismiss Charges Against Students Who Disrupted Class," Arizona State Legislature News Release, April 23, 2019.

55 Bernadette Mayer, "Failures in Infinitives," *A Bernadette Mayer Reader*, (New Directions, 1992), 139.

56 Curt Prendergast,"Federal judge in Tucson sets deadline for final arguments in border aid trial," *Arizona Daily Star*, (May 9, 2019): web.

57 Brenna Bailey, "Desert View students protest Border Patrol detainment of classmate weeks away from graduation," *Arizona Daily Star*, (May 7, 2019): web.

58 Alicia A. Caldwell and Louise Radnofsky, "US Arrests Record Number of Families at Southern Border," *Wall Street Journal*, (March 5, 2019): web.

59 "Johns Hopkins Sit-in Challenges Armed Cops, ICE Contracts," *Democracy Now*, (April 5, 2019): web.

60 Ella Torres, "Border Patrol Uninvited from community college job fair amid protests," *New York Daily News*, (April 30, 2019): web.

61 Marianna Ariel, email message to the author, Aug 8, 2019.

RESOURCES, QUESTIONS, EXERCISES

What systems or/and histories
structure your poetics?
What grammars or psychologies?
What desire(s) do you have for
your readers?
What desires do you have for yourselves
What procedures propel you?
What genealogies?
What's in your peripheral vision?
What's in your blind spot?

1. DOCUMENTARY RESOURCES

The term documentary poetry can be used to describe work that "(1) contains quotations from or reproductions of documents or statements not produced by the poet and (2) relates historical narratives, whether macro or micro, human or natural" according to poet/critic Joseph Harrington. While documentary poetry has precursors dating back centuries, many of its most famous examples were written in the first half of the twentieth century such as Ezra Pound's *Cantos*, William Carlos Williams' *Patterson*, Charles Reznikoff's *Testimony*, Charles Olson's *The Maximus Poems*, and (of course) Muriel Rukeyser's "The Book of the Dead," which predates many of these canonical examples of documentary poetry as well as anticipates continued innovation in the field.

An overview of documentary poetics as well as additional writing on the subject can be found in these texts, some of which have been referenced in this book:

"Docupoetry and Archive Desire," by Joseph Harrington. *Jacket2*, October 27, 2011.

"Against Witness" by Cathy Park Hong. *Poetry*, May 1, 2015.

"The Weight of What's Left Out: Six Contemporary Erasurists on Their Craft" by Andrew David King. *The Kenyon Review Blog*, November 6, 2012.

"From Reznikoff to Public Enemy" by Philip Metres. *Poetry Foundation*, September 22, 2008.

"Writing is Never by Itself Alone: Six Mini-Essays on Relational Investigative Poetics" by Kristin Prevallet. *Fence*, Spring 2003, 19–31.

"Creativity and the Fully Developed Bard" by Ed Sanders. *Disembodied Poetics: The Annals of the Jack Kerouac School*, ed. Anne Waldman and Andrew Schelling. Albuquerque, New Mexico: Univ of New Mexico Press, 1994, 238–269.

"The Near Transitive Properties of the Political and Poetical: Erasure," by Solmaz Sharif. *Evening Will Come: A Monthly Journal of Poetics*, April 2013.

A List Of Documentary Works Or Documentary Inspired Works Mentioned Or Discussed Within

Agee, James and Walker Evans. *Let Us Now Praise Famous Men; Three Tenant Families*. Boston: Mariner Books, 2001.

Conrad, C. A. *Ecodeviance: (Soma)tics for the Future Wilderness*. Seattle: Wave Books, 2014.

Coultas, Brenda. *A Handmade Museum: Poems*. Minneapolis: Coffee House Press, 2003.

Electronic Disturbance Theater. *Transborder Immigrant Tool/La herramienta transfronteriza para inmigrantes*. Ann Arbor, Michigan: The Office of Net Assessment, 2014.

García Manríquez, Hugo. *Anti-Humboldt: A Reading of the North American Free Trade Agreement*. Brooklyn, NY: Litmus Press, 2015.

Kapil, Bhanu. *Ban en Banlieue*. New York: Nightboat, 2015.

Little, Margaree. *Rest*. New York: Four Way Books, 2018.

Liu, Kenji. *Craters a field guide*. Goodmorning Menagerie, 2017.

Long Soldier, Layli. *Whereas*. Minneapolis: Graywolf Press, 2017.

Mayer, Bernadette. *Midwinter Day*. New York: New Directions, 1999.

Metres, Philip. *Sand Opera*. Farmington: Alice James Books, 2015.

Nowak, Mark. *Social Poetics*. Minneapolis: Coffee House Press, 2020.

Philip, M. NourbeSe. *Zong! as Told to the Author by Setaey Adamu Boateng*. Middletown: Wesleyan Univ. Press, 2008.

Rankine, Claudia. *Citizen: An American Lyric*. Minneapolis: Graywolf Press, 2014.

Rukeyser, Muriel. *The Book of the Dead*. Morgantown: Univ of West Virginia Press, 2018.

Saterstrom, Selah. *Ideal Suggestions: Essays in Divinatory Poetics*. Essay Press, 2017.

Sharif, Solmaz. *Look: Poems*. Minneapolis: Graywolf Press, 2016.

Tamayo, Jennif(f)er. *to kill the future in the present*. Chicago: Green Lantern Press, 2018.

Wright, CD. *One Big Self*. Port Townsend: Copper Canyon Press, 2007.

Vicuña, Cecilia. *The Precarious/QUIPOem: The Art and Poetry of Cecilia Vicuña*, Middletown: Wesleyan Univ. Press, 1997.

Zamora, Javier. *Unaccompanied*. Port Townsend, Washington: Copper Canyon Press, 2017.

2. QUESTIONS AND PROVOCATIONS FOR THE DOCUMENTARIAN

An Autolocation Exercise

Place yourself in the center of this box.

Now place a point on a paper to represent your subject matter.

Draw your links to your subject matter. Map your intersections.

With what kind of ruler should you scale your proximity?

Where were you born and where did the world rise up for you? What history falls behind you like a shadow? How are you writing in relation to your history? In hush, in slur, in scream?

What does your complete project look like on the shelf, screen, book, web?

What words does it sound out? Words carry shadows and histories, a whole etymology scrolling behind them. Do you know them?

Could you do this work anonymously? Collaboratively? Do you need to sign your name at all? Can you imagine a book comprised of everything written in this moment, broader than any margin? How can you gesture toward that book in your writing?

If your subject matter represents a crisis or problem, draw a version of the future without it. If you cannot see this future, you might not be ready to write.

IIII

Questions From My Documentary Poetics Students:

On Witnessing
What did you see?

___

___

___

___

___

When does witnessing become voyeurism?

___

___

___

___

How can you avoid the performance of "watch me witnessing"?

___

___

___

Is this your story to tell? Does your historical position mean that your retelling of this story reaffirms traditional routes of colonial appropriation?

___

Why tell it?

___

___

___

How can you utilize silence or represent that which is beyond representation?

___

___

___

How will you write through archives that don't exist?

___

___

___

On Ruinwork

In describing Doris Salcedo's sculptures (chairs encased in poured concrete) that formed part of her inquiry "Against Witness," Cathy Park Hong disrupts a privileged view of documenting and more importantly of witnessing. She quotes Andreas Huyssen who explains: "Everything is stored in the cloud. There is endless memory. From the point of view of the archive, forgetting is the ultimate transgression."

Hong both opens and concludes by reflecting on Salcedo's installations in terms of ruins. She approaches them as objects from an Other, who can never be accessed. It's the "infinite proximity" between viewer and Other that ignites feeling or meaning in this work, Hong concludes. She explains: "I can never metabolize what you went through, yet I cannot escape your disquieting sadness, the burden of your solitude. How it unfolds even when I leave this space. What has become of you? What could have gone through your mind?"

What ruins are you writing through or writing with?

Is your poem/project a haunting of that ruin? Why or why not?

Is your poem/project a reconstruction or a renovation? Why or why not?

Are you making a monument or defacing a monument through your poem/project?

Close your eyes as you consider an answer to this last question: if you were to be able to walk away from this ruin and never return, what world (or "utopia") would you be walking into? Would it be whole? Would it be whole with or without you?

3. FURTHER EXERCISES

Write a 12-line rhythmically charged poem in which you slant rhyme (at least twice) the name of the last official indicted from the Trump administration. Reference the most recent climate-change related disaster. Address by first name one of the 24 migrants who have died in ICE custody since 2017. End with the instructions given to you by a parent or guardian on what you should do when waking from a nightmare.

IIII

Write a poem as an acrostic of the name of a person you love who is most vulnerable to US government policies. Include a quote (unattributed) from a writer killed by an authoritarian regime or a line in which you complete the phrase:

"I have birthed ________________ and buried ________________."

End with a line that snaps like a turnstile at your back, that closes like an iron gate behind you.

IIII

Typographically represent the 650 miles of border wall teetering on the 2000-mile US-Mexico boundary. Write a 3-word refrain that could be used as a chant to tear the shroud of normalcy. Answer the question: What brought your parents to the place they birthed you? End with a line so open it would allow both a child and an endangered Mexican gray wolf to step through.

IIII

Begin with the city from which you write. Use your five senses to describe the most recently gentrified neighborhood. Personify a "For Sale" sign or an underfunded public school. Do not include an image of a transient.

IIII

Write a 48-line poem in which each line ends with you claiming "executive privilege" or some variation of that phrase. Answer the question: What do you call someone who cannot speak and comes without a name? Reference the last time you were terrified by a cop.

End with a metaphor that gasps for air or water

or end with a couplet that screeches like a line drawn in the dirt.

IIII

Write a poem that binds you and your reader as tightly as the zip ties encircling protestors' wrists. Use empathy, compassion, complicity. Include the all reasons why you have not placed your body in the streets or the courts to protect the person you love who is most vulnerable to the state. Address that person. End with a line that moans like gas entering your tank or end with a line that divides nothing.

IIII

In couplets, describe the opening shot of a movie you would make to depict the events of the past year. Slant rhyme the name of at least one known Russian hacking virus. Describe a monument, then deface it.

End by completing the phrase:

I would ________ 2000 miles to end ____________.

IIII

Write a poem that records all the new developments that have occurred in our country's continued assault on migrants and/or other nonwhite bodies while you were writing any one of the above poems.

IIII

Make a list of words that sound like shots being fired on a residential street or that sound like children being herded into cages. Create a poem around these words. It should not rhyme.

IIII

Print this on the lightest paper, on the newsprint we used for practicing our letters in elementary school, paper dissolving under our spit and erasures.

Build a wall of file cabinets
then burn them.

LIST OF IMAGES, ACKNOWLEDGMENTS

LIST OF IMAGES

Frames, Erasures, Graffiti

Page 13, Tucson Operation Streamline Calendar

Pages 14–15, Border wall, Nogales, Sonora (credit Sophia Terazawa)

Page 23, Map and spread sheet depicting the number of remains found in the desert (from the Arizona OpenGIS Initiative for Deceased Migrants and available through the Humane Borders website)

Page 24, collage by Susan Briante

Pages 28–29, from *Whereas* by Layli Long Solidier, pages 83 and 85

Page 33, designed by Suzi Garcia

Writing in Relation

Page 43, Article from the *Los Angeles Times* on the naturalization ceremony in which Farid and his aunts participated

Pages 44–45, Alien Registration card, Anna Brianti

Page 52, Google map of the Tohono O'odham Nation, Map Data © 2020 Google

Page 57, Baptism Certificate (in Italian) for Geraldo Brianti from St. Lucy's Church, Newark, NJ

Guidestars, Tangles, Hauntologies

Pages 78–79, Water station south of Tucson (credit Raquel Gutiérrez)

Page 80, Water station south of Tucson (credit Raquel Gutiérrez)

Page 81, Page from the "Desert Survival Series" as published in the *Transborder Immigrant Tool/La herramienta transfronteriza para inmigrantes*

Page 91, from *Zong!* by M. NourbeSe Phillip, page 3

Page 100, from the Juan Basco Migrant Shelter in Nogales, Sonora (credit Sophia Terazawa)

Page 105, from Ana Teresa Fernández's website (credit Maria Teresa Fernández)

Epilogue: Stopped Clocks, Rolling Videos

Page 113, Photo of my mother's dresser on the day she died and handwritten list of objects on my mother's nightstand on the day she died

Page 116, Image from Amy Siskind's Twitter feed (Week 2)

Pages 120–121, Image from Timothy Snyder's Facebook page (November 15, 2016), an excerpt of the full list posted that day

Page 124, Case Summary Report, University of Arizona Police Department

Page 129, from The Report on the Investigation into Russian Interference in the 2016 Presidential Election, (the Mueller Report) (redacted) page 52

Page 130, "Drop the Charges Against the Arizona 3" call-in campaign jpeg shared on social media

Resources, Questions, and Exercises

Page 141, White Board from my documentary poetics graduate seminar

ACKNOWLEDGMENTS

Grateful acknowledgment is given to the editors of *Fence* magazine's on-line portal and *The Brooklyn Rail*, where excerpts from this book first appeared.

Some of my previously published essays also informed the thinking in this book. I offer my gratitude to the editors of these publications for providing the space and, often, the feedback with which to develop these ideas:

"Big Data, Bird Song." *The Manifesto Project*. Eds. Rebecca Hazelton and Alan Michael Parker. Akron, OH: University of Akron Press, 2016. 48–51.

"Defacing the Monument: Rukeyser's Innovations in Docupoetics." *Jacket 2 (online)*, April 21, 2014.

"Seeing and Gathering: Cecilia Vicuña." *The Texas Observer*, May 21, 2004: 24–26.

"The New Political." *Pilot Light Journal (online)*, December 2012.

"Then Burn." *A Dozen Nothing (online)*, April 2017.

"We Need More than Stories for the Unheard." *High Country News*, Nov. 11, 2019.

IIII

A book is always a collaborative effort. I offer my deepest gratitude to many people, especially:

To those friends and colleagues whose readings of this text and conversations about some of the issues included within informed this work: Rosa Alcalá, R. Bruno, Jenny Browne, Marianna Ariel, Todd Fredson, Carmen Giménez Smith, Jen Hofer, J. Michael Martínez, Farid Matuk, Ander Monson, Metta Sáma, and Sarah Vap.

To the participants in the University of Arizona Creative Writing MFA program's Southwest Field Studies in Writing Program: Emilio Carrero, Abby Dockter, Gabe Dozal, Lee Anne Gallaway, Raquel Gutiérrez, Katerina Ivanov, Logan Phillips, Sophia Terazawa, and Miranda Trimmier; to our community partners at the Borderlands Restoration Network, the Kino Border Initiative, Humane Borders and the Borderlands Community Alliance. **If you are moved by what you have read here, please consider donating to these groups** and others (such as No More Deaths and the Florence Project), who are working for environmental and social justice on the US-Mexico border.

Special gratitude to the Agnese Nelms Haury Program in Environment and Social Justice and Alison Deming for supporting the Southwest Field Studies in Writing Program from 2017-2019.

Special gratitude to the Ucross Foundation Residency Program for the space and time to develop this work.

To the graduate students in my documentary arts classes at the University of Arizona and my colleagues in the English Department, especially in the MFA in Creative Writing program.

To Sarah Gzemski, Emily Alex, and Douglas Kearney at Noemi Press. Special gratitude and love to Suzi F. Garcia and Carmen Giménez Smith for their brilliant counsel and support in helping me bring this book into print.

On the occasion of her most recent publication, the poet and essayist Anne Boyer tweeted: "That a book is the work of only its author is always a lie...Find your crew and make it the world." To Rosa Alcalá, Carmen Giménez Smith and Stephanie Pearmain—for being the crew that sustained me.

To Gianna—for inspiring me to continue to work towards a better world and for making the world better by her presence.

In *The Life of Poetry*, Muriel Rukeyser writes "In a time of suffering, long war, and the opening of the horizon, there is no resource which we can afford to overlook or to misunderstand." She then goes on to write about love and poetry.

To Farid Matuk—endless gratitude for both.

ABOUT THE AUTHOR

Susan Briante is the author of three books of poetry: *Pioneers in the Study of Motion*, *Utopia Minus*, and *The Market Wonders*, all from Ahsahta Press. She is a professor of creative writing at the University of Arizona, where she also serves as co-coordinator of the Southwest Field Studies in Writing Program. The program brings MFA students to the US-Mexico border to engage in reciprocal writing and research projects with community-based environmental and social justice groups.